W9-APT-128

Table of Contents

How to Use This Book

More Minute Math Drills: Multiplication and Division is designed to help students build math fluency in just minutes each day. Each student's objective is to complete one drill page with 100% accuracy within a given time period.

This teacher-friendly book features four types of worksheets to help students who learn at different rates. There are drill pages with 30 problems that provide students with a challenging review. Drill pages with 60 and 72 problems are divided with cut lines after 20 or 24 problems. Each of these pages can be used as one drill page or cut apart for students who need to focus on a small number of problems. Students should not be timed when the page is cut apart. Activity worksheets reinforce the skills being taught in an easy-to-understand and entertaining format.

Make a copy of the Multiplication and Division Table on page 5 for each student to reference before completing drill pages.

Use the following suggested time limits for students to complete one drill page. Each suggested time limit may be adjusted to meet students' needs.

Third grade: 3–5 minutes
Fourth grade: 2–4 minutes
Fifth and sixth grades: 1–3 minutes

Before beginning, tell students the amount of time they have to complete the worksheet. Have each student mark the time at the top of her drill page as shown. Note: These minute bubbles only appear on drill pages.

Minutes

Tell students when to begin and when to stop. Then, have students exchange papers and mark any incorrect answers as you read the answers aloud. Do not give credit for incomplete answers. An answer key is provided on pages 122–128 to assist with assessment. Write each student's grade as a percentage or a fraction in the score bubble at the top of her drill page. Round scores if necessary.

93%
Score

28/30
Score

Grades may be recorded on the Score Sheet on page 6. Make a copy for each student and ask her to keep track of her scores. This sheet will motivate students to beat their previous scores.

You may award students with certificates after they master each skill. Award certificates are provided on pages 7 and 8.

MORE Minute Math Drills

MULTIPLICATION & DIVISION

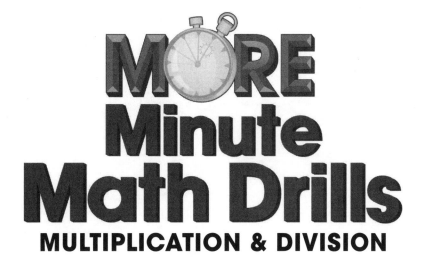

Carson-Dellosa Publishing Company, Inc.

Greensboro, North Carolina

Credits

Editor: Barrie Hoople

Layout Design: Lori Jackson and Julie Kinlaw

Cover Design: Lori Jackson

Cover Illustration: Ray Lambert

ISBN: 978-1-60418-036-7
11-195201151

Multiplication and Division Table

X/÷	0	1	2	3	4	5	6	7	8	9	10	11	12
0	0	0	0	0	0	0	0	0	0	0	0	0	0
1	0	1	2	3	4	5	6	7	8	9	10	11	12
2	0	2	4	6	8	10	12	14	16	18	20	22	24
3	0	3	6	9	12	15	18	21	24	27	30	33	36
4	0	4	8	12	16	20	24	28	32	36	40	44	48
5	0	5	10	15	20	25	30	35	40	45	50	55	60
6	0	6	12	18	24	30	36	42	48	54	60	66	72
7	0	7	14	21	28	35	42	49	56	63	70	77	84
8	0	8	16	24	32	40	48	56	64	72	80	88	96
9	0	9	18	27	36	45	54	63	72	81	90	99	108
10	0	10	20	30	40	50	60	70	80	90	100	110	120
11	0	11	22	33	44	55	66	77	88	99	110	121	132
12	0	12	24	36	48	60	72	84	96	108	120	132	144

To use the Multiplication and Division Table to multiply, pick two numbers to multiply. Find the first factor in the left column. Slide your finger across that row until you are in the column of the second factor. The number in this box is the product. For example, if you are multiplying 5 x 4, start at 5 in the left column. Slide your finger across from 5 until it is even with 4 in the top column. The product is 20.

To use the Multiplication and Division Table to divide, pick two numbers to divide. Find the divisor in the left column. Slide your finger across the row to the dividend. Then, slide your finger up from the dividend to the top row. The number in this box is the quotient. For example, if you are dividing 63 by 7, find 7 in the left column and slide your finger across to 63. Then, slide your finger up from 63 to the top row. The quotient is 9.

SCORE SHEET

Name _____

Page	Time	0–69	70	71	72	73	74	75	76	77	78	79	80	81	82	83	84	85	86	87	88	89	90	91	92	93	94	95	96	97	98	99	100

Certificate
of
ACHIEVEMENT

Name

This certificate is presented

for attaining 100% accuracy

within a _____ minute time limit

on More Minute Math drills!

Certificate
of
ACHIEVEMENT

Name

This certificate is presented

for attaining 100% accuracy

within a _____ minute time limit

on More Minute Math drills!

Fast Facts Award

_____

has demonstrated the ability
to think quickly and accurately
when working _____ problems.

Signature: _____

Date: _____

Fast Facts Award

_____

has demonstrated the ability
to think quickly and accurately
when working _____ problems.

Signature: _____

Date: _____

Score

Multiplying 10

1 2 3 4 5
Minutes

A. 10   10   10   10   10   10   10   10   12   10
   x 2   x 5   x 3   x 1   x 9   x 0   x 11   x 4   x 10   x 6

B. 10   10   11   10   10   10   10   10   10   10
   x 8   x 10   x 10   x 7   x 12   x 1   x 8   x 0   x 3   x 5

C. 10   12   10   10   10   10   10   10   11   10
   x 7   x 10   x 11   x 1   x 9   x 4   x 2   x 6   x 10   x 0

D. 10   10   10   10   10   10   10   12   10   10
  x 12   x 4   x 10   x 9   x 3   x 2   x 8   x 10   x 7   x 5

E. 10   10   10   10   10   10   10   10   11   10
   x 3   x 5   x 12   x 6   x 11   x 0   x 6   x 8   x 10   x 1

F. 10   10   11   12   10   10   10   10   10   10
   x 4   x 2   x 10   x 10   x 5   x 7   x 9   x 10   x 3   x 8

Multiplying 10

Solve each problem.

A.
   10   10   10   10   10
  x 0   x 12   x 1   x 10   x 3

B.
   10   10   10   10   10
  x 4   x 6   x 8   x 1   x 2

C.
   10   10   10   12   10
  x 5   x 9   x 4   x 10   x 6

D.
   10   10   11   10   10
  x 7   x 2   x 10   x 8   x 4

E.
   10   10   10   10   10
  x 11   x 5   x 3   x 12   x 7

F.
   10   10   10   10   11
  x 9   x 10   x 6   x 8   x 10

Mixed Review

A.
$\begin{array}{r} 2 \\ \times 9 \\ \hline \end{array}$
$\begin{array}{r} 0 \\ \times 0 \\ \hline \end{array}$
$\begin{array}{r} 5 \\ \times 2 \\ \hline \end{array}$
$\begin{array}{r} 12 \\ \times 1 \\ \hline \end{array}$
$\begin{array}{r} 10 \\ \times 9 \\ \hline \end{array}$
$\begin{array}{r} 12 \\ \times 5 \\ \hline \end{array}$
$\begin{array}{r} 2 \\ \times 7 \\ \hline \end{array}$
$\begin{array}{r} 8 \\ \times 5 \\ \hline \end{array}$
$\begin{array}{r} 1 \\ \times 6 \\ \hline \end{array}$
$\begin{array}{r} 11 \\ \times 10 \\ \hline \end{array}$

B.
$\begin{array}{r} 0 \\ \times 9 \\ \hline \end{array}$
$\begin{array}{r} 10 \\ \times 4 \\ \hline \end{array}$
$\begin{array}{r} 6 \\ \times 2 \\ \hline \end{array}$
$\begin{array}{r} 6 \\ \times 5 \\ \hline \end{array}$
$\begin{array}{r} 0 \\ \times 7 \\ \hline \end{array}$
$\begin{array}{r} 3 \\ \times 2 \\ \hline \end{array}$
$\begin{array}{r} 10 \\ \times 7 \\ \hline \end{array}$
$\begin{array}{r} 5 \\ \times 5 \\ \hline \end{array}$
$\begin{array}{r} 12 \\ \times 0 \\ \hline \end{array}$
$\begin{array}{r} 7 \\ \times 5 \\ \hline \end{array}$

C.
$\begin{array}{r} 10 \\ \times 0 \\ \hline \end{array}$
$\begin{array}{r} 11 \\ \times 1 \\ \hline \end{array}$
$\begin{array}{r} 8 \\ \times 2 \\ \hline \end{array}$
$\begin{array}{r} 12 \\ \times 10 \\ \hline \end{array}$
$\begin{array}{r} 4 \\ \times 1 \\ \hline \end{array}$
$\begin{array}{r} 12 \\ \times 2 \\ \hline \end{array}$
$\begin{array}{r} 4 \\ \times 5 \\ \hline \end{array}$
$\begin{array}{r} 5 \\ \times 9 \\ \hline \end{array}$
$\begin{array}{r} 11 \\ \times 0 \\ \hline \end{array}$
$\begin{array}{r} 4 \\ \times 2 \\ \hline \end{array}$

D.
$\begin{array}{r} 1 \\ \times 9 \\ \hline \end{array}$
$\begin{array}{r} 3 \\ \times 5 \\ \hline \end{array}$
$\begin{array}{r} 10 \\ \times 10 \\ \hline \end{array}$
$\begin{array}{r} 6 \\ \times 0 \\ \hline \end{array}$
$\begin{array}{r} 9 \\ \times 5 \\ \hline \end{array}$
$\begin{array}{r} 10 \\ \times 11 \\ \hline \end{array}$
$\begin{array}{r} 2 \\ \times 6 \\ \hline \end{array}$
$\begin{array}{r} 5 \\ \times 0 \\ \hline \end{array}$
$\begin{array}{r} 2 \\ \times 3 \\ \hline \end{array}$
$\begin{array}{r} 10 \\ \times 5 \\ \hline \end{array}$

E.
$\begin{array}{r} 3 \\ \times 1 \\ \hline \end{array}$
$\begin{array}{r} 10 \\ \times 0 \\ \hline \end{array}$
$\begin{array}{r} 10 \\ \times 1 \\ \hline \end{array}$
$\begin{array}{r} 2 \\ \times 5 \\ \hline \end{array}$
$\begin{array}{r} 5 \\ \times 7 \\ \hline \end{array}$
$\begin{array}{r} 2 \\ \times 2 \\ \hline \end{array}$
$\begin{array}{r} 1 \\ \times 3 \\ \hline \end{array}$
$\begin{array}{r} 4 \\ \times 1 \\ \hline \end{array}$
$\begin{array}{r} 7 \\ \times 0 \\ \hline \end{array}$
$\begin{array}{r} 10 \\ \times 12 \\ \hline \end{array}$

F.
$\begin{array}{r} 9 \\ \times 1 \\ \hline \end{array}$
$\begin{array}{r} 1 \\ \times 7 \\ \hline \end{array}$
$\begin{array}{r} 0 \\ \times 6 \\ \hline \end{array}$
$\begin{array}{r} 10 \\ \times 2 \\ \hline \end{array}$
$\begin{array}{r} 5 \\ \times 3 \\ \hline \end{array}$
$\begin{array}{r} 2 \\ \times 8 \\ \hline \end{array}$
$\begin{array}{r} 6 \\ \times 1 \\ \hline \end{array}$
$\begin{array}{r} 0 \\ \times 5 \\ \hline \end{array}$
$\begin{array}{r} 11 \\ \times 5 \\ \hline \end{array}$
$\begin{array}{r} 8 \\ \times 1 \\ \hline \end{array}$

A. 10   9   0   11   5   12   5   10   0   10
    x7   x2   x8   x1   x6   x10   x7   x10   x4   x3

B. 9   12   10   7   10   6   2   8   5   11
    x5   x5   x0   x5   x12   x0   x3   x5   x2   x0

- -

C. 2   6   5   3   10   4   10   0   12   10
    x6   x1   x0   x5   x12   x2   x5   x6   x2   x6

D. 2   10   11   2   11   5   4   10   3   7
    x5   x1   x5   x1   x2   x6   x5   x2   x2   x5

- -

E. 10   1   2   0   5   6   8   2   10   5
    x11   x1   x7   x5   x8   x5   x2   x9   x9   x1

F. 6   10   2   1   5   12   11   1   10   10
    x2   x0   x2   x8   x5   x5   x10   x3   x6   x8

Multiplying 3

A.
$\begin{array}{r} 0 \\ \times 3 \\ \hline \end{array}$
$\begin{array}{r} 3 \\ \times 3 \\ \hline \end{array}$
$\begin{array}{r} 4 \\ \times 3 \\ \hline \end{array}$
$\begin{array}{r} 3 \\ \times 0 \\ \hline \end{array}$
$\begin{array}{r} 1 \\ \times 3 \\ \hline \end{array}$
$\begin{array}{r} 6 \\ \times 3 \\ \hline \end{array}$
$\begin{array}{r} 3 \\ \times 7 \\ \hline \end{array}$
$\begin{array}{r} 10 \\ \times 3 \\ \hline \end{array}$
$\begin{array}{r} 5 \\ \times 3 \\ \hline \end{array}$
$\begin{array}{r} 3 \\ \times 4 \\ \hline \end{array}$

B.
$\begin{array}{r} 8 \\ \times 3 \\ \hline \end{array}$
$\begin{array}{r} 3 \\ \times 6 \\ \hline \end{array}$
$\begin{array}{r} 11 \\ \times 3 \\ \hline \end{array}$
$\begin{array}{r} 2 \\ \times 3 \\ \hline \end{array}$
$\begin{array}{r} 3 \\ \times 8 \\ \hline \end{array}$
$\begin{array}{r} 7 \\ \times 3 \\ \hline \end{array}$
$\begin{array}{r} 12 \\ \times 3 \\ \hline \end{array}$
$\begin{array}{r} 3 \\ \times 2 \\ \hline \end{array}$
$\begin{array}{r} 9 \\ \times 3 \\ \hline \end{array}$
$\begin{array}{r} 3 \\ \times 1 \\ \hline \end{array}$

C.
$\begin{array}{r} 3 \\ \times 5 \\ \hline \end{array}$
$\begin{array}{r} 3 \\ \times 9 \\ \hline \end{array}$
$\begin{array}{r} 5 \\ \times 3 \\ \hline \end{array}$
$\begin{array}{r} 3 \\ \times 0 \\ \hline \end{array}$
$\begin{array}{r} 12 \\ \times 3 \\ \hline \end{array}$
$\begin{array}{r} 4 \\ \times 3 \\ \hline \end{array}$
$\begin{array}{r} 3 \\ \times 8 \\ \hline \end{array}$
$\begin{array}{r} 0 \\ \times 3 \\ \hline \end{array}$
$\begin{array}{r} 6 \\ \times 3 \\ \hline \end{array}$
$\begin{array}{r} 3 \\ \times 5 \\ \hline \end{array}$

D.
$\begin{array}{r} 3 \\ \times 3 \\ \hline \end{array}$
$\begin{array}{r} 7 \\ \times 3 \\ \hline \end{array}$
$\begin{array}{r} 3 \\ \times 1 \\ \hline \end{array}$
$\begin{array}{r} 2 \\ \times 3 \\ \hline \end{array}$
$\begin{array}{r} 3 \\ \times 6 \\ \hline \end{array}$
$\begin{array}{r} 1 \\ \times 3 \\ \hline \end{array}$
$\begin{array}{r} 11 \\ \times 3 \\ \hline \end{array}$
$\begin{array}{r} 8 \\ \times 3 \\ \hline \end{array}$
$\begin{array}{r} 3 \\ \times 4 \\ \hline \end{array}$
$\begin{array}{r} 9 \\ \times 3 \\ \hline \end{array}$

E.
$\begin{array}{r} 3 \\ \times 7 \\ \hline \end{array}$
$\begin{array}{r} 10 \\ \times 3 \\ \hline \end{array}$
$\begin{array}{r} 3 \\ \times 0 \\ \hline \end{array}$
$\begin{array}{r} 3 \\ \times 3 \\ \hline \end{array}$
$\begin{array}{r} 12 \\ \times 3 \\ \hline \end{array}$
$\begin{array}{r} 4 \\ \times 3 \\ \hline \end{array}$
$\begin{array}{r} 8 \\ \times 3 \\ \hline \end{array}$
$\begin{array}{r} 3 \\ \times 4 \\ \hline \end{array}$
$\begin{array}{r} 1 \\ \times 3 \\ \hline \end{array}$
$\begin{array}{r} 11 \\ \times 3 \\ \hline \end{array}$

F.
$\begin{array}{r} 3 \\ \times 2 \\ \hline \end{array}$
$\begin{array}{r} 6 \\ \times 3 \\ \hline \end{array}$
$\begin{array}{r} 3 \\ \times 8 \\ \hline \end{array}$
$\begin{array}{r} 3 \\ \times 7 \\ \hline \end{array}$
$\begin{array}{r} 10 \\ \times 3 \\ \hline \end{array}$
$\begin{array}{r} 3 \\ \times 6 \\ \hline \end{array}$
$\begin{array}{r} 9 \\ \times 3 \\ \hline \end{array}$
$\begin{array}{r} 0 \\ \times 3 \\ \hline \end{array}$
$\begin{array}{r} 11 \\ \times 3 \\ \hline \end{array}$
$\begin{array}{r} 3 \\ \times 9 \\ \hline \end{array}$

Multiplying 3

Solve each problem. Draw a line from each boxcar to the engine with the matching product.

A.
3 x 1 =

18

B.
2 x 3 =

36

C.
6 x 3 =

3

D.
12 x 3 =

6

E.
3 x 9 =

21

F.
7 x 3 =

27

G.
5 x 3 =

30

H.
10 x 3 =

15

I.
11 x 3 =

12

J.
3 x 0 =

33

K.
3 x 3 =

9

L.
3 x 4 =

0

Mixed Review

A.
0	5	9	2	10	3	1	5	8	11
$\times 1$	$\times 1$	$\times 2$	$\times 3$	$\times 1$	$\times 3$	$\times 7$	$\times 6$	$\times 3$	$\times 1$

B.
2	5	1	0	3	12	2	8	7	11
$\times 7$	$\times 9$	$\times 5$	$\times 7$	$\times 7$	$\times 10$	$\times 5$	$\times 5$	$\times 3$	$\times 10$

C.
7	12	5	11	6	8	9	10	12	7
$\times 2$	$\times 0$	$\times 8$	$\times 6$	$\times 4$	$\times 0$	$\times 9$	$\times 3$	$\times 6$	$\times 6$

D.
9	3	11	6	12	2	6	3	4	7
$\times 4$	$\times 5$	$\times 3$	$\times 7$	$\times 5$	$\times 0$	$\times 6$	$\times 2$	$\times 3$	$\times 5$

E.
8	11	10	5	7	1	9	3	6	11
$\times 6$	$\times 5$	$\times 10$	$\times 0$	$\times 9$	$\times 1$	$\times 7$	$\times 9$	$\times 8$	$\times 2$

F.
2	8	12	5	10	6	9	3	6	5
$\times 2$	$\times 9$	$\times 9$	$\times 5$	$\times 0$	$\times 9$	$\times 8$	$\times 4$	$\times 3$	$\times 7$

1 2 3 4 5
Minutes

Mixed Review

Score

A. 10   5   1   4   3   4   1   11   0   2
   x 1   x 7   x 3   x 2   x 3   x 0   x 8   x 1   x 6   x 9

B.   8   7   9   7   5   3   7   6   3   10
   x 2   x 9   x 1   x 5   x 9   x 5   x 6   x 8   x 6   x 12

C.   9   11   3   5   11   4   2   7   3   0
   x 6   x 2   x 7   x 8   x 5   x 5   x 1   x 9   x 4   x 9

D.   6   3   12   10   12   1   3   6   2   11
   x 4   x 8   x 2   x 1   x 9   x 8   x 3   x 5   x 5   x 3

E.   9   11   9   2   10   3   7   6   6   12
   x 5   x 10   x 9   x 8   x 10   x 8   x 3   x 7   x 8   x 5

F.   9   8   1   2   6   5   0   12   10   7
   x 6   x 9   x 2   x 4   x 6   x 4   x 8   x 10   x 1   x 0

Name: _____   Date: _____

Multiplying 4

A. $\begin{array}{r}4\\ \times 8\\ \hline\end{array}$ $\begin{array}{r}9\\ \times 4\\ \hline\end{array}$ $\begin{array}{r}4\\ \times 4\\ \hline\end{array}$ $\begin{array}{r}3\\ \times 4\\ \hline\end{array}$ $\begin{array}{r}4\\ \times 9\\ \hline\end{array}$ $\begin{array}{r}4\\ \times 1\\ \hline\end{array}$ $\begin{array}{r}6\\ \times 4\\ \hline\end{array}$ $\begin{array}{r}10\\ \times 4\\ \hline\end{array}$ $\begin{array}{r}12\\ \times 4\\ \hline\end{array}$ $\begin{array}{r}4\\ \times 6\\ \hline\end{array}$

B. $\begin{array}{r}2\\ \times 4\\ \hline\end{array}$ $\begin{array}{r}1\\ \times 4\\ \hline\end{array}$ $\begin{array}{r}4\\ \times 0\\ \hline\end{array}$ $\begin{array}{r}10\\ \times 4\\ \hline\end{array}$ $\begin{array}{r}5\\ \times 4\\ \hline\end{array}$ $\begin{array}{r}2\\ \times 4\\ \hline\end{array}$ $\begin{array}{r}4\\ \times 3\\ \hline\end{array}$ $\begin{array}{r}7\\ \times 4\\ \hline\end{array}$ $\begin{array}{r}8\\ \times 4\\ \hline\end{array}$ $\begin{array}{r}11\\ \times 4\\ \hline\end{array}$

- -

C. $\begin{array}{r}4\\ \times 5\\ \hline\end{array}$ $\begin{array}{r}1\\ \times 4\\ \hline\end{array}$ $\begin{array}{r}4\\ \times 4\\ \hline\end{array}$ $\begin{array}{r}3\\ \times 4\\ \hline\end{array}$ $\begin{array}{r}4\\ \times 4\\ \hline\end{array}$ $\begin{array}{r}4\\ \times 1\\ \hline\end{array}$ $\begin{array}{r}7\\ \times 4\\ \hline\end{array}$ $\begin{array}{r}12\\ \times 4\\ \hline\end{array}$ $\begin{array}{r}6\\ \times 4\\ \hline\end{array}$ $\begin{array}{r}2\\ \times 4\\ \hline\end{array}$

D. $\begin{array}{r}4\\ \times 0\\ \hline\end{array}$ $\begin{array}{r}12\\ \times 4\\ \hline\end{array}$ $\begin{array}{r}5\\ \times 4\\ \hline\end{array}$ $\begin{array}{r}4\\ \times 2\\ \hline\end{array}$ $\begin{array}{r}4\\ \times 3\\ \hline\end{array}$ $\begin{array}{r}4\\ \times 8\\ \hline\end{array}$ $\begin{array}{r}4\\ \times 7\\ \hline\end{array}$ $\begin{array}{r}11\\ \times 4\\ \hline\end{array}$ $\begin{array}{r}4\\ \times 9\\ \hline\end{array}$ $\begin{array}{r}0\\ \times 4\\ \hline\end{array}$

- -

E. $\begin{array}{r}4\\ \times 6\\ \hline\end{array}$ $\begin{array}{r}11\\ \times 4\\ \hline\end{array}$ $\begin{array}{r}1\\ \times 4\\ \hline\end{array}$ $\begin{array}{r}8\\ \times 4\\ \hline\end{array}$ $\begin{array}{r}2\\ \times 4\\ \hline\end{array}$ $\begin{array}{r}4\\ \times 9\\ \hline\end{array}$ $\begin{array}{r}11\\ \times 4\\ \hline\end{array}$ $\begin{array}{r}1\\ \times 4\\ \hline\end{array}$ $\begin{array}{r}0\\ \times 4\\ \hline\end{array}$ $\begin{array}{r}12\\ \times 4\\ \hline\end{array}$

F. $\begin{array}{r}4\\ \times 4\\ \hline\end{array}$ $\begin{array}{r}4\\ \times 5\\ \hline\end{array}$ $\begin{array}{r}4\\ \times 8\\ \hline\end{array}$ $\begin{array}{r}4\\ \times 0\\ \hline\end{array}$ $\begin{array}{r}6\\ \times 4\\ \hline\end{array}$ $\begin{array}{r}9\\ \times 4\\ \hline\end{array}$ $\begin{array}{r}4\\ \times 3\\ \hline\end{array}$ $\begin{array}{r}7\\ \times 4\\ \hline\end{array}$ $\begin{array}{r}10\\ \times 4\\ \hline\end{array}$ $\begin{array}{r}4\\ \times 4\\ \hline\end{array}$

Multiplying 4

Solve each problem. Circle the largest product to find which car wins the race.

A.

4	2	6	5	4	7	12
x1	x4	x4	x4	x9	x4	x4

B.

10	11	4	4	7	3	6
x4	x4	x2	x5	x4	x4	x4

C.

8	4	4	9	4	4	1
x4	x5	x0	x4	x6	x8	x4

D.

2	4	4	11	4	6	5
x4	x4	x3	x4	x7	x4	x4

E.

10	8	4	4	4	4	9
x4	x4	x4	x0	x2	x5	x4

F.

11	7	0	4	2	10	6
x4	x4	x4	x3	x4	x4	x4

Score

Multiplying 7

1 2 3 4 5
Minutes

A. 7   0   1   3   7   12   4   7   7   8
   x 2   x 7   x 7   x 7   x 5   x 7   x 7   x 3   x 1   x 7

B. 11   7   5   7   9   10   7   7   7   7
   x 7   x 4   x 7   x 0   x 7   x 7   x 9   x 6   x 7   x 8

C. 6   7   0   7   12   7   7   9   5   7
   x 7   x 7   x 7   x 9   x 7   x 1   x 2   x 7   x 7   x 3

D. 7   11   7   8   7   10   7   3   2   1
   x 4   x 7   x 5   x 7   x 0   x 7   x 6   x 7   x 7   x 7

E. 7   7   4   8   12   7   7   10   6   11
   x 8   x 7   x 7   x 7   x 7   x 0   x 6   x 7   x 7   x 7

F. 7   9   7   7   7   1   0   7   7   2
   x 3   x 7   x 7   x 2   x 5   x 7   x 7   x 1   x 4   x 7

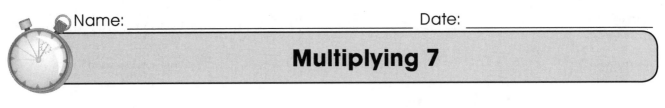

Multiplying 7

Solve each problem.

A. 0 x 7 =

B. 7 x 4 =

C. 6 x 7 =

D. 7 x 1 =

E. 3 x 7 =

F. 10 x 7 =

G. 7 x 9 =

H. 7 x 2 =

I. 7 x 3 =

J. 7 x 8 =

K. 9 x 7 =

L. 7 x 7 =

M. 5 x 7 =

N. 7 x 11 =

O. 7 x 6 =

P. 12 x 7 =

Q. 7 x 0 =

R. 5 x 7 =

S. 11 x 7 =

T. 4 x 7 =

U. 7 x 12 =

V. 2 x 7 =

W. 1 x 7 =

X. 8 x 7 =

Mixed Review

A.
$$\begin{array}{r}0\\ \times 9\\ \hline\end{array}\quad\begin{array}{r}6\\ \times 0\\ \hline\end{array}\quad\begin{array}{r}7\\ \times 2\\ \hline\end{array}\quad\begin{array}{r}8\\ \times 1\\ \hline\end{array}\quad\begin{array}{r}10\\ \times 9\\ \hline\end{array}\quad\begin{array}{r}12\\ \times 5\\ \hline\end{array}\quad\begin{array}{r}2\\ \times 9\\ \hline\end{array}\quad\begin{array}{r}8\\ \times 5\\ \hline\end{array}\quad\begin{array}{r}4\\ \times 6\\ \hline\end{array}\quad\begin{array}{r}10\\ \times 8\\ \hline\end{array}$$

B.
$$\begin{array}{r}7\\ \times 9\\ \hline\end{array}\quad\begin{array}{r}11\\ \times 6\\ \hline\end{array}\quad\begin{array}{r}12\\ \times 3\\ \hline\end{array}\quad\begin{array}{r}6\\ \times 8\\ \hline\end{array}\quad\begin{array}{r}12\\ \times 7\\ \hline\end{array}\quad\begin{array}{r}4\\ \times 2\\ \hline\end{array}\quad\begin{array}{r}10\\ \times 10\\ \hline\end{array}\quad\begin{array}{r}5\\ \times 5\\ \hline\end{array}\quad\begin{array}{r}12\\ \times 0\\ \hline\end{array}\quad\begin{array}{r}7\\ \times 5\\ \hline\end{array}$$

C.
$$\begin{array}{r}0\\ \times 3\\ \hline\end{array}\quad\begin{array}{r}11\\ \times 1\\ \hline\end{array}\quad\begin{array}{r}11\\ \times 2\\ \hline\end{array}\quad\begin{array}{r}4\\ \times 7\\ \hline\end{array}\quad\begin{array}{r}1\\ \times 0\\ \hline\end{array}\quad\begin{array}{r}12\\ \times 2\\ \hline\end{array}\quad\begin{array}{r}6\\ \times 5\\ \hline\end{array}\quad\begin{array}{r}4\\ \times 9\\ \hline\end{array}\quad\begin{array}{r}7\\ \times 7\\ \hline\end{array}\quad\begin{array}{r}9\\ \times 1\\ \hline\end{array}$$

D.
$$\begin{array}{r}1\\ \times 5\\ \hline\end{array}\quad\begin{array}{r}3\\ \times 5\\ \hline\end{array}\quad\begin{array}{r}10\\ \times 4\\ \hline\end{array}\quad\begin{array}{r}7\\ \times 0\\ \hline\end{array}\quad\begin{array}{r}9\\ \times 5\\ \hline\end{array}\quad\begin{array}{r}10\\ \times 12\\ \hline\end{array}\quad\begin{array}{r}2\\ \times 6\\ \hline\end{array}\quad\begin{array}{r}8\\ \times 0\\ \hline\end{array}\quad\begin{array}{r}8\\ \times 3\\ \hline\end{array}\quad\begin{array}{r}10\\ \times 5\\ \hline\end{array}$$

E.
$$\begin{array}{r}3\\ \times 1\\ \hline\end{array}\quad\begin{array}{r}10\\ \times 11\\ \hline\end{array}\quad\begin{array}{r}10\\ \times 3\\ \hline\end{array}\quad\begin{array}{r}4\\ \times 5\\ \hline\end{array}\quad\begin{array}{r}6\\ \times 7\\ \hline\end{array}\quad\begin{array}{r}12\\ \times 2\\ \hline\end{array}\quad\begin{array}{r}2\\ \times 3\\ \hline\end{array}\quad\begin{array}{r}4\\ \times 1\\ \hline\end{array}\quad\begin{array}{r}1\\ \times 1\\ \hline\end{array}\quad\begin{array}{r}10\\ \times 6\\ \hline\end{array}$$

F.
$$\begin{array}{r}11\\ \times 9\\ \hline\end{array}\quad\begin{array}{r}8\\ \times 7\\ \hline\end{array}\quad\begin{array}{r}11\\ \times 0\\ \hline\end{array}\quad\begin{array}{r}10\\ \times 2\\ \hline\end{array}\quad\begin{array}{r}5\\ \times 2\\ \hline\end{array}\quad\begin{array}{r}2\\ \times 8\\ \hline\end{array}\quad\begin{array}{r}12\\ \times 8\\ \hline\end{array}\quad\begin{array}{r}0\\ \times 2\\ \hline\end{array}\quad\begin{array}{r}11\\ \times 4\\ \hline\end{array}\quad\begin{array}{r}6\\ \times 1\\ \hline\end{array}$$

Mixed Review

A.   3   10   0   9   10   3   2   10   7   1
    x 4   x 6   x 5   x 7   x 1   x 3   x 8   x 5   x 5   x 3

B.   9   12   10   12   10   9   6   2   12   11
    x 8   x 4   x 10   x 5   x 12   x 0   x 3   x 5   x 7   x 3

- -

C.   7   0   7   3   12   12   4   4   7   2
    x 6   x 1   x 2   x 9   x 1   x 7   x 3   x 8   x 9   x 3

D.   3   9   7   8   12   1   3   12   10   8
    x 6   x 4   x 3   x 9   x 6   x 7   x 9   x 4   x 4   x 5

- -

E. 12   2   8   5   8   2   12   11   10   4
    x 3   x 2   x 7   x 5   x 6   x 9   x 8   x 7   x 2   x 7

F.   6   8   10   11   7   5   8   4   7   10
    x 9   x 8   x 8   x 3   x 1   x 5   x 3   x 4   x 5   x 1

Multiplying 11

Score

1 2 3 4 5
Minutes

A.
$\begin{array}{r} 11 \\ \times 6 \\ \hline \end{array}$
$\begin{array}{r} 11 \\ \times 5 \\ \hline \end{array}$
$\begin{array}{r} 11 \\ \times 0 \\ \hline \end{array}$
$\begin{array}{r} 11 \\ \times 4 \\ \hline \end{array}$
$\begin{array}{r} 11 \\ \times 2 \\ \hline \end{array}$
$\begin{array}{r} 11 \\ \times 6 \\ \hline \end{array}$
$\begin{array}{r} 11 \\ \times 3 \\ \hline \end{array}$
$\begin{array}{r} 11 \\ \times 4 \\ \hline \end{array}$
$\begin{array}{r} 11 \\ \times 7 \\ \hline \end{array}$
$\begin{array}{r} 11 \\ \times 1 \\ \hline \end{array}$

B.
$\begin{array}{r} 11 \\ \times 7 \\ \hline \end{array}$
$\begin{array}{r} 11 \\ \times 9 \\ \hline \end{array}$
$\begin{array}{r} 11 \\ \times 2 \\ \hline \end{array}$
$\begin{array}{r} 11 \\ \times 5 \\ \hline \end{array}$
$\begin{array}{r} 11 \\ \times 8 \\ \hline \end{array}$
$\begin{array}{r} 11 \\ \times 0 \\ \hline \end{array}$
$\begin{array}{r} 11 \\ \times 1 \\ \hline \end{array}$
$\begin{array}{r} 11 \\ \times 8 \\ \hline \end{array}$
$\begin{array}{r} 11 \\ \times 9 \\ \hline \end{array}$
$\begin{array}{r} 11 \\ \times 3 \\ \hline \end{array}$

C.
$\begin{array}{r} 11 \\ \times 7 \\ \hline \end{array}$
$\begin{array}{r} 11 \\ \times 1 \\ \hline \end{array}$
$\begin{array}{r} 11 \\ \times 3 \\ \hline \end{array}$
$\begin{array}{r} 11 \\ \times 6 \\ \hline \end{array}$
$\begin{array}{r} 11 \\ \times 9 \\ \hline \end{array}$
$\begin{array}{r} 11 \\ \times 6 \\ \hline \end{array}$
$\begin{array}{r} 11 \\ \times 2 \\ \hline \end{array}$
$\begin{array}{r} 11 \\ \times 7 \\ \hline \end{array}$
$\begin{array}{r} 11 \\ \times 0 \\ \hline \end{array}$
$\begin{array}{r} 12 \\ \times 11 \\ \hline \end{array}$

D.
$\begin{array}{r} 11 \\ \times 8 \\ \hline \end{array}$
$\begin{array}{r} 11 \\ \times 10 \\ \hline \end{array}$
$\begin{array}{r} 11 \\ \times 5 \\ \hline \end{array}$
$\begin{array}{r} 11 \\ \times 8 \\ \hline \end{array}$
$\begin{array}{r} 11 \\ \times 11 \\ \hline \end{array}$
$\begin{array}{r} 11 \\ \times 0 \\ \hline \end{array}$
$\begin{array}{r} 11 \\ \times 5 \\ \hline \end{array}$
$\begin{array}{r} 11 \\ \times 12 \\ \hline \end{array}$
$\begin{array}{r} 11 \\ \times 11 \\ \hline \end{array}$
$\begin{array}{r} 11 \\ \times 4 \\ \hline \end{array}$

E.
$\begin{array}{r} 11 \\ \times 6 \\ \hline \end{array}$
$\begin{array}{r} 11 \\ \times 10 \\ \hline \end{array}$
$\begin{array}{r} 11 \\ \times 1 \\ \hline \end{array}$
$\begin{array}{r} 10 \\ \times 11 \\ \hline \end{array}$
$\begin{array}{r} 11 \\ \times 9 \\ \hline \end{array}$
$\begin{array}{r} 11 \\ \times 3 \\ \hline \end{array}$
$\begin{array}{r} 11 \\ \times 2 \\ \hline \end{array}$
$\begin{array}{r} 11 \\ \times 3 \\ \hline \end{array}$
$\begin{array}{r} 11 \\ \times 1 \\ \hline \end{array}$
$\begin{array}{r} 11 \\ \times 7 \\ \hline \end{array}$

F.
$\begin{array}{r} 11 \\ \times 4 \\ \hline \end{array}$
$\begin{array}{r} 11 \\ \times 12 \\ \hline \end{array}$
$\begin{array}{r} 11 \\ \times 8 \\ \hline \end{array}$
$\begin{array}{r} 11 \\ \times 5 \\ \hline \end{array}$
$\begin{array}{r} 11 \\ \times 2 \\ \hline \end{array}$
$\begin{array}{r} 12 \\ \times 11 \\ \hline \end{array}$
$\begin{array}{r} 11 \\ \times 0 \\ \hline \end{array}$
$\begin{array}{r} 11 \\ \times 11 \\ \hline \end{array}$
$\begin{array}{r} 11 \\ \times 7 \\ \hline \end{array}$
$\begin{array}{r} 11 \\ \times 4 \\ \hline \end{array}$

Multiplying 11

Solve each problem. Circle the largest product to find which ship arrives first.

A.

11	11	11	11	11	11	11
x 9	x 0	x 2	x 4	x 7	x 3	x 8

B.

11	11	11	11	11	11	11
x 2	x 11	x 3	x 4	x 6	x 10	x 5

C.

11	11	11	11	11	11	12
x 1	x 7	x 9	x 0	x 2	x 8	x 11

D.

11	11	11	11	11	11	11
x 6	x 8	x 2	x 4	x 9	x 10	x 1

E.

11	11	11	11	11	11	11
x 0	x 5	x 10	x 6	x 3	x 4	x 7

F.

11	11	11	10	11	11	11
x 11	x 2	x 9	x 11	x 1	x 6	x 4

Multiplying 12

A.
$$\begin{array}{r} 12 \\ \times 10 \\ \hline \end{array}$$
$$\begin{array}{r} 12 \\ \times 3 \\ \hline \end{array}$$
$$\begin{array}{r} 10 \\ \times 12 \\ \hline \end{array}$$
$$\begin{array}{r} 12 \\ \times 0 \\ \hline \end{array}$$
$$\begin{array}{r} 12 \\ \times 5 \\ \hline \end{array}$$
$$\begin{array}{r} 12 \\ \times 9 \\ \hline \end{array}$$
$$\begin{array}{r} 12 \\ \times 12 \\ \hline \end{array}$$
$$\begin{array}{r} 12 \\ \times 8 \\ \hline \end{array}$$
$$\begin{array}{r} 12 \\ \times 2 \\ \hline \end{array}$$
$$\begin{array}{r} 12 \\ \times 4 \\ \hline \end{array}$$

B.
$$\begin{array}{r} 12 \\ \times 4 \\ \hline \end{array}$$
$$\begin{array}{r} 12 \\ \times 5 \\ \hline \end{array}$$
$$\begin{array}{r} 12 \\ \times 2 \\ \hline \end{array}$$
$$\begin{array}{r} 12 \\ \times 1 \\ \hline \end{array}$$
$$\begin{array}{r} 11 \\ \times 12 \\ \hline \end{array}$$
$$\begin{array}{r} 12 \\ \times 7 \\ \hline \end{array}$$
$$\begin{array}{r} 12 \\ \times 8 \\ \hline \end{array}$$
$$\begin{array}{r} 12 \\ \times 9 \\ \hline \end{array}$$
$$\begin{array}{r} 12 \\ \times 6 \\ \hline \end{array}$$
$$\begin{array}{r} 12 \\ \times 11 \\ \hline \end{array}$$

C.
$$\begin{array}{r} 12 \\ \times 5 \\ \hline \end{array}$$
$$\begin{array}{r} 12 \\ \times 2 \\ \hline \end{array}$$
$$\begin{array}{r} 12 \\ \times 3 \\ \hline \end{array}$$
$$\begin{array}{r} 12 \\ \times 8 \\ \hline \end{array}$$
$$\begin{array}{r} 12 \\ \times 0 \\ \hline \end{array}$$
$$\begin{array}{r} 12 \\ \times 9 \\ \hline \end{array}$$
$$\begin{array}{r} 11 \\ \times 12 \\ \hline \end{array}$$
$$\begin{array}{r} 12 \\ \times 7 \\ \hline \end{array}$$
$$\begin{array}{r} 12 \\ \times 6 \\ \hline \end{array}$$
$$\begin{array}{r} 12 \\ \times 0 \\ \hline \end{array}$$

D.
$$\begin{array}{r} 12 \\ \times 6 \\ \hline \end{array}$$
$$\begin{array}{r} 12 \\ \times 1 \\ \hline \end{array}$$
$$\begin{array}{r} 12 \\ \times 4 \\ \hline \end{array}$$
$$\begin{array}{r} 12 \\ \times 12 \\ \hline \end{array}$$
$$\begin{array}{r} 12 \\ \times 5 \\ \hline \end{array}$$
$$\begin{array}{r} 12 \\ \times 7 \\ \hline \end{array}$$
$$\begin{array}{r} 11 \\ \times 12 \\ \hline \end{array}$$
$$\begin{array}{r} 12 \\ \times 1 \\ \hline \end{array}$$
$$\begin{array}{r} 12 \\ \times 2 \\ \hline \end{array}$$
$$\begin{array}{r} 12 \\ \times 9 \\ \hline \end{array}$$

E.
$$\begin{array}{r} 12 \\ \times 12 \\ \hline \end{array}$$
$$\begin{array}{r} 12 \\ \times 0 \\ \hline \end{array}$$
$$\begin{array}{r} 12 \\ \times 1 \\ \hline \end{array}$$
$$\begin{array}{r} 12 \\ \times 11 \\ \hline \end{array}$$
$$\begin{array}{r} 12 \\ \times 3 \\ \hline \end{array}$$
$$\begin{array}{r} 12 \\ \times 1 \\ \hline \end{array}$$
$$\begin{array}{r} 12 \\ \times 6 \\ \hline \end{array}$$
$$\begin{array}{r} 12 \\ \times 7 \\ \hline \end{array}$$
$$\begin{array}{r} 12 \\ \times 3 \\ \hline \end{array}$$
$$\begin{array}{r} 12 \\ \times 8 \\ \hline \end{array}$$

F.
$$\begin{array}{r} 12 \\ \times 9 \\ \hline \end{array}$$
$$\begin{array}{r} 12 \\ \times 7 \\ \hline \end{array}$$
$$\begin{array}{r} 11 \\ \times 12 \\ \hline \end{array}$$
$$\begin{array}{r} 12 \\ \times 5 \\ \hline \end{array}$$
$$\begin{array}{r} 12 \\ \times 6 \\ \hline \end{array}$$
$$\begin{array}{r} 12 \\ \times 0 \\ \hline \end{array}$$
$$\begin{array}{r} 12 \\ \times 4 \\ \hline \end{array}$$
$$\begin{array}{r} 10 \\ \times 12 \\ \hline \end{array}$$
$$\begin{array}{r} 12 \\ \times 2 \\ \hline \end{array}$$
$$\begin{array}{r} 12 \\ \times 12 \\ \hline \end{array}$$

Multiplying 12

Solve each problem.

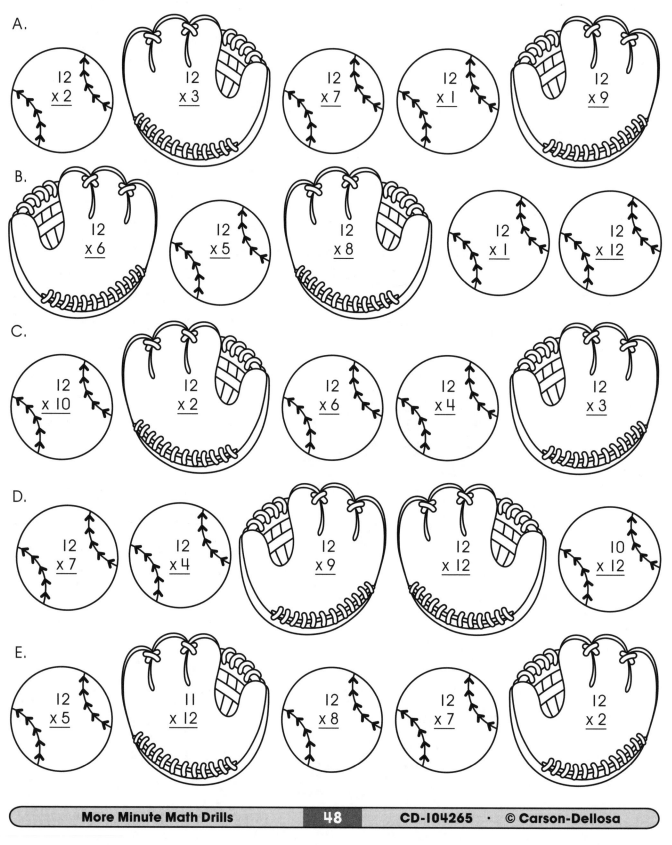

A.
12
x 2

12
x 3

12
x 7

12
x 1

12
x 9

B.
12
x 6

12
x 5

12
x 8

12
x 1

12
x 12

C.
12
x 10

12
x 2

12
x 6

12
x 4

12
x 3

D.
12
x 7

12
x 4

12
x 9

12
x 12

10
x 12

E.
12
x 5

11
x 12

12
x 8

12
x 7

12
x 2

Multiplying 11 and 12

1 2 3 4 5
Minutes

A. 11 x 7 =   2 x 12 =   5 x 11 =   12 x 0 =   12 x 9 =

    11 x 10 =   12 x 12 =   3 x 11 =   11 x 0 =   6 x 12 =

B. 2 x 11 =   8 x 11 =   12 x 5 =   12 x 3 =   11 x 4 =

    11 x 1 =   12 x 1 =   7 x 12 =   12 x 11 =   10 x 12 =

C. 11 x 6 =   9 x 11 =   8 x 12 =   3 x 12 =   4 x 12 =

    12 x 8 =   11 x 3 =   11 x 11 =   0 x 12 =   11 x 2 =

D. 7 x 11 =   9 x 12 =   12 x 12 =   10 x 11 =   11 x 8 =

    11 x 5 =   1 x 12 =   12 x 7 =   12 x 10 =   12 x 11 =

E. 11 x 9 =   12 x 6 =   8 x 12 =   5 x 12 =   12 x 2 =

    6 x 11 =   4 x 11 =   12 x 4 =   12 x 10 =   11 x 5 =

F. 10 x 11 =   12 x 2 =   11 x 12 =   1 x 11 =   11 x 11 =

    11 x 0 =   12 x 4 =   8 x 11 =   12 x 1 =   11 x 7 =

1 2 3 4 5
Minutes

Multiplying 11 and 12

Score

A.	12 x 6	11 x 12	11 x 7	11 x 6	12 x 9
B.	12 x 8	12 x 6	11 x 3	12 x 7	11 x 10
C.	11 x 11	12 x 8	11 x 7	10 x 12	12 x 9
D.	11 x 4	12 x 1	10 x 11	11 x 0	12 x 2
E.	12 x 5	11 x 1	11 x 5	12 x 6	12 x 3
F.	11 x 2	12 x 4	11 x 8	12 x 11	11 x 9

Mixed Review

A.   7   5   6   12   6   7   12   11   12   9
   x6   x5   x2   x3   x3   x4   x8   x2   x4   x9

B.   1   2   11   3   2   9   1   8   9   0
   x0   x3   x1   x0   x9   x1   x3   x9   x4   x0

C.   1   5   8   3   6   10   8   8   10   7
   x2   x1   x5   x3   x5   x5   x7   x4   x4   x0

D.   11   5   11   0   4   12   10   10   4   0
   x0   x4   x5   x6   x2   x6   x6   x7   x4   x5

E.   8   10   5   9   6   8   10   10   8   12
   x3   x2   x2   x3   x6   x2   x0   x11   x8   x0

F.   0   10   0   9   11   12   9   3   11   10
   x4   x3   x8   x7   x3   x1   x0   x4   x7   x8

Mixed Review

A. 0   1   7   12   1   2   10   7   2   9
   x5   x8   x2   x0   x1   x7   x2   x1   x2   x0

B. 1   2   1   11   2   4   3   8   3   2
   x0   x8   x6   x1   x0   x1   x2   x0   x1   x9

C. 11   5   2   2   8   6   8   0   6   1
   x0   x1   x4   x2   x2   x0   x1   x3   x2   x5

D. 12   0   1   2   0   9   1   1   6   12
   x2   x4   x2   x5   x0   x1   x4   x2   x1   x1

E. 2   2   5   0   4   10   12   11   3   10
   x6   x1   x2   x6   x2   x0   x1   x2   x0   x1

F. 0   12   0   11   1   9   9   1   11   2
   x7   x0   x9   x1   x3   x2   x1   x7   x4   x3

Mixed Review

Score

1 2 3 4 5
Minutes

A.
$$\begin{array}{r} 4 \\ \times 7 \\ \hline \end{array}$$
$$\begin{array}{r} 5 \\ \times 7 \\ \hline \end{array}$$
$$\begin{array}{r} 7 \\ \times 3 \\ \hline \end{array}$$
$$\begin{array}{r} 12 \\ \times 4 \\ \hline \end{array}$$
$$\begin{array}{r} 6 \\ \times 3 \\ \hline \end{array}$$
$$\begin{array}{r} 10 \\ \times 5 \\ \hline \end{array}$$
$$\begin{array}{r} 9 \\ \times 5 \\ \hline \end{array}$$
$$\begin{array}{r} 12 \\ \times 3 \\ \hline \end{array}$$
$$\begin{array}{r} 3 \\ \times 8 \\ \hline \end{array}$$
$$\begin{array}{r} 5 \\ \times 2 \\ \hline \end{array}$$

B.
$$\begin{array}{r} 11 \\ \times 3 \\ \hline \end{array}$$
$$\begin{array}{r} 3 \\ \times 0 \\ \hline \end{array}$$
$$\begin{array}{r} 4 \\ \times 5 \\ \hline \end{array}$$
$$\begin{array}{r} 4 \\ \times 8 \\ \hline \end{array}$$
$$\begin{array}{r} 3 \\ \times 2 \\ \hline \end{array}$$
$$\begin{array}{r} 12 \\ \times 5 \\ \hline \end{array}$$
$$\begin{array}{r} 0 \\ \times 4 \\ \hline \end{array}$$
$$\begin{array}{r} 9 \\ \times 4 \\ \hline \end{array}$$
$$\begin{array}{r} 5 \\ \times 6 \\ \hline \end{array}$$
$$\begin{array}{r} 5 \\ \times 4 \\ \hline \end{array}$$

C.
$$\begin{array}{r} 8 \\ \times 4 \\ \hline \end{array}$$
$$\begin{array}{r} 5 \\ \times 1 \\ \hline \end{array}$$
$$\begin{array}{r} 7 \\ \times 4 \\ \hline \end{array}$$
$$\begin{array}{r} 2 \\ \times 3 \\ \hline \end{array}$$
$$\begin{array}{r} 11 \\ \times 5 \\ \hline \end{array}$$
$$\begin{array}{r} 4 \\ \times 9 \\ \hline \end{array}$$
$$\begin{array}{r} 11 \\ \times 4 \\ \hline \end{array}$$
$$\begin{array}{r} 5 \\ \times 3 \\ \hline \end{array}$$
$$\begin{array}{r} 8 \\ \times 5 \\ \hline \end{array}$$
$$\begin{array}{r} 8 \\ \times 3 \\ \hline \end{array}$$

D.
$$\begin{array}{r} 3 \\ \times 3 \\ \hline \end{array}$$
$$\begin{array}{r} 4 \\ \times 4 \\ \hline \end{array}$$
$$\begin{array}{r} 0 \\ \times 5 \\ \hline \end{array}$$
$$\begin{array}{r} 4 \\ \times 3 \\ \hline \end{array}$$
$$\begin{array}{r} 12 \\ \times 4 \\ \hline \end{array}$$
$$\begin{array}{r} 5 \\ \times 7 \\ \hline \end{array}$$
$$\begin{array}{r} 1 \\ \times 3 \\ \hline \end{array}$$
$$\begin{array}{r} 12 \\ \times 5 \\ \hline \end{array}$$
$$\begin{array}{r} 4 \\ \times 6 \\ \hline \end{array}$$
$$\begin{array}{r} 6 \\ \times 0 \\ \hline \end{array}$$

E.
$$\begin{array}{r} 5 \\ \times 8 \\ \hline \end{array}$$
$$\begin{array}{r} 7 \\ \times 5 \\ \hline \end{array}$$
$$\begin{array}{r} 3 \\ \times 3 \\ \hline \end{array}$$
$$\begin{array}{r} 11 \\ \times 5 \\ \hline \end{array}$$
$$\begin{array}{r} 2 \\ \times 5 \\ \hline \end{array}$$
$$\begin{array}{r} 10 \\ \times 4 \\ \hline \end{array}$$
$$\begin{array}{r} 3 \\ \times 5 \\ \hline \end{array}$$
$$\begin{array}{r} 10 \\ \times 3 \\ \hline \end{array}$$
$$\begin{array}{r} 5 \\ \times 5 \\ \hline \end{array}$$
$$\begin{array}{r} 10 \\ \times 6 \\ \hline \end{array}$$

F.
$$\begin{array}{r} 0 \\ \times 6 \\ \hline \end{array}$$
$$\begin{array}{r} 4 \\ \times 2 \\ \hline \end{array}$$
$$\begin{array}{r} 11 \\ \times 4 \\ \hline \end{array}$$
$$\begin{array}{r} 1 \\ \times 4 \\ \hline \end{array}$$
$$\begin{array}{r} 9 \\ \times 3 \\ \hline \end{array}$$
$$\begin{array}{r} 4 \\ \times 4 \\ \hline \end{array}$$
$$\begin{array}{r} 5 \\ \times 7 \\ \hline \end{array}$$
$$\begin{array}{r} 12 \\ \times 3 \\ \hline \end{array}$$
$$\begin{array}{r} 2 \\ \times 4 \\ \hline \end{array}$$
$$\begin{array}{r} 4 \\ \times 0 \\ \hline \end{array}$$

Mixed Review

A.
$$\begin{array}{c}4\\ \times 4\end{array}\quad\begin{array}{c}5\\ \times 5\end{array}\quad\begin{array}{c}6\\ \times 3\end{array}\quad\begin{array}{c}0\\ \times 0\end{array}\quad\begin{array}{c}1\\ \times 3\end{array}\quad\begin{array}{c}12\\ \times 5\end{array}\quad\begin{array}{c}0\\ \times 2\end{array}\quad\begin{array}{c}5\\ \times 1\end{array}\quad\begin{array}{c}0\\ \times 9\end{array}\quad\begin{array}{c}7\\ \times 5\end{array}$$

B.
$$\begin{array}{c}12\\ \times 4\end{array}\quad\begin{array}{c}12\\ \times 1\end{array}\quad\begin{array}{c}10\\ \times 2\end{array}\quad\begin{array}{c}5\\ \times 3\end{array}\quad\begin{array}{c}5\\ \times 6\end{array}\quad\begin{array}{c}8\\ \times 5\end{array}\quad\begin{array}{c}2\\ \times 4\end{array}\quad\begin{array}{c}10\\ \times 4\end{array}\quad\begin{array}{c}11\\ \times 2\end{array}\quad\begin{array}{c}6\\ \times 0\end{array}$$

C.
$$\begin{array}{c}11\\ \times 4\end{array}\quad\begin{array}{c}1\\ \times 1\end{array}\quad\begin{array}{c}2\\ \times 4\end{array}\quad\begin{array}{c}3\\ \times 2\end{array}\quad\begin{array}{c}1\\ \times 2\end{array}\quad\begin{array}{c}12\\ \times 3\end{array}\quad\begin{array}{c}8\\ \times 3\end{array}\quad\begin{array}{c}8\\ \times 2\end{array}\quad\begin{array}{c}4\\ \times 0\end{array}\quad\begin{array}{c}3\\ \times 9\end{array}$$

D.
$$\begin{array}{c}11\\ \times 0\end{array}\quad\begin{array}{c}7\\ \times 1\end{array}\quad\begin{array}{c}9\\ \times 2\end{array}\quad\begin{array}{c}2\\ \times 5\end{array}\quad\begin{array}{c}3\\ \times 3\end{array}\quad\begin{array}{c}2\\ \times 7\end{array}\quad\begin{array}{c}3\\ \times 4\end{array}\quad\begin{array}{c}0\\ \times 3\end{array}\quad\begin{array}{c}4\\ \times 1\end{array}\quad\begin{array}{c}3\\ \times 5\end{array}$$

E.
$$\begin{array}{c}7\\ \times 0\end{array}\quad\begin{array}{c}4\\ \times 8\end{array}\quad\begin{array}{c}4\\ \times 3\end{array}\quad\begin{array}{c}11\\ \times 3\end{array}\quad\begin{array}{c}2\\ \times 8\end{array}\quad\begin{array}{c}3\\ \times 9\end{array}\quad\begin{array}{c}12\\ \times 0\end{array}\quad\begin{array}{c}11\\ \times 1\end{array}\quad\begin{array}{c}7\\ \times 5\end{array}\quad\begin{array}{c}4\\ \times 9\end{array}$$

F.
$$\begin{array}{c}6\\ \times 5\end{array}\quad\begin{array}{c}7\\ \times 4\end{array}\quad\begin{array}{c}1\\ \times 9\end{array}\quad\begin{array}{c}0\\ \times 5\end{array}\quad\begin{array}{c}10\\ \times 5\end{array}\quad\begin{array}{c}0\\ \times 2\end{array}\quad\begin{array}{c}4\\ \times 1\end{array}\quad\begin{array}{c}2\\ \times 2\end{array}\quad\begin{array}{c}9\\ \times 5\end{array}\quad\begin{array}{c}10\\ \times 1\end{array}$$

Mixed Review

A.
12	4	11	7	1	11	7	8	3	6
x 6	x 6	x 7	x 8	x 6	x 8	x 0	x 5	x 7	x 9

B.
3	8	12	1	10	11	8	8	12	2
x 6	x 3	x 8	x 8	x 6	x 6	x 0	x 6	x 7	x 8

- -

C.
10	10	7	8	9	4	7	1	11	7
x 6	x 7	x 7	x 1	x 6	x 8	x 5	x 6	x 6	x 3

D.
8	7	6	7	7	8	6	0	12	7
x 9	x 2	x 6	x 4	x 9	x 8	x 7	x 8	x 8	x 8

- -

E.
5	6	1	8	0	5	11	6	5	3
x 6	x 6	x 8	x 8	x 8	x 7	x 7	x 3	x 8	x 8

F.
8	6	2	1	8	6	11	0	9	6
x 7	x 4	x 6	x 7	x 2	x 1	x 8	x 6	x 7	x 8

1 2 3 4 5
Minutes

Mixed Review

Score

A. 9   12   9   12   11   3   10   1   9   2
   x0   x9   x5   x0   x3   x9   x7   x9   x4   x9

B. 9   11   10   11   11   10   12   12   10   8
   x9   x0   x6   x4   x11   x1   x6   x7   x8   x9

- -

C. 11   12   12   10   11   12   12   12   12   10
   x1   x10   x4   x2   x6   x8   x7   x5   x3   x7

D. 10   12   10   7   10   11   12   11   12   12
   x4   x12   x5   x9   x3   x2   x2   x9   x0   x1

- -

E. 10   11   10   9   11   11   10   5   10   11
   x9   x11   x11   x1   x4   x7   x3   x9   x0   x6

F. 9   12   11   11   9   10   12   11   10   9
   x6   x8   x5   x8   x3   x10   x9   x12   x5   x9

Mixed Review

A.
$\begin{array}{r} 6 \\ \times\, 0 \\ \hline \end{array}$
$\begin{array}{r} 9 \\ \times\, 7 \\ \hline \end{array}$
$\begin{array}{r} 3 \\ \times\, 7 \\ \hline \end{array}$
$\begin{array}{r} 11 \\ \times\, 8 \\ \hline \end{array}$
$\begin{array}{r} 10 \\ \times\, 9 \\ \hline \end{array}$
$\begin{array}{r} 9 \\ \times\, 1 \\ \hline \end{array}$
$\begin{array}{r} 9 \\ \times\, 5 \\ \hline \end{array}$
$\begin{array}{r} 6 \\ \times\, 6 \\ \hline \end{array}$
$\begin{array}{r} 12 \\ \times\, 0 \\ \hline \end{array}$
$\begin{array}{r} 12 \\ \times\, 8 \\ \hline \end{array}$

B.
$\begin{array}{r} 11 \\ \times\, 5 \\ \hline \end{array}$
$\begin{array}{r} 6 \\ \times\, 4 \\ \hline \end{array}$
$\begin{array}{r} 10 \\ \times\, 6 \\ \hline \end{array}$
$\begin{array}{r} 11 \\ \times\, 6 \\ \hline \end{array}$
$\begin{array}{r} 12 \\ \times\, 4 \\ \hline \end{array}$
$\begin{array}{r} 8 \\ \times\, 3 \\ \hline \end{array}$
$\begin{array}{r} 6 \\ \times\, 7 \\ \hline \end{array}$
$\begin{array}{r} 11 \\ \times\, 11 \\ \hline \end{array}$
$\begin{array}{r} 10 \\ \times\, 1 \\ \hline \end{array}$
$\begin{array}{r} 12 \\ \times\, 6 \\ \hline \end{array}$

- -

C.
$\begin{array}{r} 7 \\ \times\, 8 \\ \hline \end{array}$
$\begin{array}{r} 11 \\ \times\, 8 \\ \hline \end{array}$
$\begin{array}{r} 10 \\ \times\, 3 \\ \hline \end{array}$
$\begin{array}{r} 10 \\ \times\, 7 \\ \hline \end{array}$
$\begin{array}{r} 7 \\ \times\, 7 \\ \hline \end{array}$
$\begin{array}{r} 12 \\ \times\, 6 \\ \hline \end{array}$
$\begin{array}{r} 2 \\ \times\, 9 \\ \hline \end{array}$
$\begin{array}{r} 12 \\ \times\, 1 \\ \hline \end{array}$
$\begin{array}{r} 8 \\ \times\, 9 \\ \hline \end{array}$
$\begin{array}{r} 6 \\ \times\, 9 \\ \hline \end{array}$

D.
$\begin{array}{r} 10 \\ \times\, 5 \\ \hline \end{array}$
$\begin{array}{r} 8 \\ \times\, 5 \\ \hline \end{array}$
$\begin{array}{r} 12 \\ \times\, 3 \\ \hline \end{array}$
$\begin{array}{r} 11 \\ \times\, 7 \\ \hline \end{array}$
$\begin{array}{r} 10 \\ \times\, 8 \\ \hline \end{array}$
$\begin{array}{r} 6 \\ \times\, 3 \\ \hline \end{array}$
$\begin{array}{r} 10 \\ \times\, 2 \\ \hline \end{array}$
$\begin{array}{r} 11 \\ \times\, 12 \\ \hline \end{array}$
$\begin{array}{r} 2 \\ \times\, 6 \\ \hline \end{array}$
$\begin{array}{r} 11 \\ \times\, 4 \\ \hline \end{array}$

- -

E.
$\begin{array}{r} 8 \\ \times\, 1 \\ \hline \end{array}$
$\begin{array}{r} 11 \\ \times\, 1 \\ \hline \end{array}$
$\begin{array}{r} 7 \\ \times\, 9 \\ \hline \end{array}$
$\begin{array}{r} 11 \\ \times\, 9 \\ \hline \end{array}$
$\begin{array}{r} 12 \\ \times\, 7 \\ \hline \end{array}$
$\begin{array}{r} 12 \\ \times\, 8 \\ \hline \end{array}$
$\begin{array}{r} 11 \\ \times\, 2 \\ \hline \end{array}$
$\begin{array}{r} 4 \\ \times\, 8 \\ \hline \end{array}$
$\begin{array}{r} 7 \\ \times\, 2 \\ \hline \end{array}$
$\begin{array}{r} 12 \\ \times\, 9 \\ \hline \end{array}$

F.
$\begin{array}{r} 12 \\ \times\, 7 \\ \hline \end{array}$
$\begin{array}{r} 12 \\ \times\, 12 \\ \hline \end{array}$
$\begin{array}{r} 7 \\ \times\, 5 \\ \hline \end{array}$
$\begin{array}{r} 11 \\ \times\, 10 \\ \hline \end{array}$
$\begin{array}{r} 8 \\ \times\, 9 \\ \hline \end{array}$
$\begin{array}{r} 10 \\ \times\, 12 \\ \hline \end{array}$
$\begin{array}{r} 9 \\ \times\, 6 \\ \hline \end{array}$
$\begin{array}{r} 10 \\ \times\, 0 \\ \hline \end{array}$
$\begin{array}{r} 5 \\ \times\, 6 \\ \hline \end{array}$
$\begin{array}{r} 10 \\ \times\, 7 \\ \hline \end{array}$

A. 7   12   2   10   6   10   1   8   12   12
   x7   x2   x0   x6   x4   x5   x3   x8   x7   x3

B. 11   2   5   10   6   5   8   12   7   2
   x5   x2   x2   x1   x6   x3   x1   x1   x1   x8

C. 5   7   4   11   3   0   12   1   0   8
   x5   x4   x5   x7   x6   x9   x7   x5   x2   x3

D. 6   4   11   0   10   4   11   6   7   7
   x8   x8   x11   x0   x2   x0   x8   x0   x9   x1

E. 1   12   0   11   1   10   3   9   10   12
   x6   x12   x4   x4   x1   x11   x3   x5   x3   x9

F. 2   9   10   11   9   9   8   5   10   3
   x6   x6   x4   x5   x0   x9   x6   x9   x1   x0

Mixed Review

A. 12   11   9   10   11   9   11   10   12   6
   x 8   x 11   x 8   x 6   x 7   x 9   x 12   x 4   x 6   x 9

B.   7   10   12   12   3   10   12   11   10   11
   x 9   x 12   x 4   x 12   x 9   x 11   x 9   x 5   x 0   x 4

- -

C. 12   12   11   2   4   12   10   11   9   8
   x 2   x 5   x 3   x 9   x 9   x 6   x 7   x 6   x 0   x 8

D.   4   4   12   12   10   11   7   8   6   10
   x 7   x 6   x 11   x 7   x 3   x 9   x 2   x 5   x 6   x 1

- -

E.   8   10   9   7   10   11   6   8   12   4
   x 4   x 8   x 5   x 7   x 9   x 0   x 2   x 2   x 4   x 2

F. 12   1   6   3   12   5   4   8   7   10
   x 3   x 7   x 4   x 9   x 6   x 5   x 4   x 5   x 9   x 6

1 2 3 4 5
Minutes

Mixed Review

Score

A. 0   8   7   4   12   5   12   10   12   10
   x 1   x 2   x 3   x 6   x 12   x 6   x 6   x 7   x 7   x 6

B. 4   10   5   12   8   6   11   9   11   11
   x 3   x 0   x 8   x 4   x 7   x 3   x 6   x 4   x 10   x 3

- -

C. 12   3   10   2   3   9   12   3   12   11
   x 6   x 3   x 7   x 1   x 5   x 2   x 5   x 2   x 7   x 5

D. 12   10   4   7   8   11   9   5   9   6
   x 6   x 10   x 7   x 6   x 3   x 7   x 3   x 2   x 5   x 5

- -

E. 12   11   2   5   7   2   3   11   10   6
   x 5   x 0   x 1   x 7   x 3   x 6   x 8   x 8   x 4   x 7

F. 5   8   10   8   7   6   12   1   7   10
   x 5   x 6   x 12   x 4   x 7   x 6   x 2   x 6   x 6   x 3

Score

Dividing by 1

A. $9 \div 1 =$ $1\overline{)4}$ $0 \div 1 =$ $1\overline{)12}$ $7 \div 1 =$

  $1\overline{)5}$ $6 \div 1 =$ $1\overline{)3}$ $11 \div 1 =$ $1\overline{)1}$

B. $2 \div 1 =$ $1\overline{)8}$ $10 \div 1 =$ $1\overline{)6}$ $4 \div 1 =$

  $1\overline{)0}$ $5 \div 1 =$ $1\overline{)11}$ $1 \div 1 =$ $1\overline{)6}$

C. $7 \div 1 =$ $1\overline{)10}$ $4 \div 1 =$ $1\overline{)7}$ $12 \div 1 =$

  $1\overline{)2}$ $5 \div 1 =$ $1\overline{)0}$ $8 \div 1 =$ $1\overline{)2}$

D. $9 \div 1 =$ $1\overline{)4}$ $2 \div 1 =$ $1\overline{)12}$ $3 \div 1 =$

  $1\overline{)7}$ $0 \div 1 =$ $1\overline{)1}$ $11 \div 1 =$ $1\overline{)3}$

E. $2 \div 1 =$ $1\overline{)8}$ $10 \div 1 =$ $1\overline{)5}$ $0 \div 1 =$

  $1\overline{)6}$ $7 \div 1 =$ $1\overline{)3}$ $9 \div 1 =$ $1\overline{)4}$

F. $3 \div 1 =$ $1\overline{)11}$ $1 \div 1 =$ $1\overline{)9}$ $6 \div 1 =$

  $1\overline{)0}$ $4 \div 1 =$ $1\overline{)10}$ $12 \div 1 =$ $1\overline{)2}$

Dividing by 1

Solve each problem.

A.   5 ÷ 1 =   0 ÷ 1 =   11 ÷ 1 =   10 ÷ 1 =   2 ÷ 1 =

B.   9 ÷ 1 =   6 ÷ 1 =   7 ÷ 1 =   3 ÷ 1 =   4 ÷ 1 =

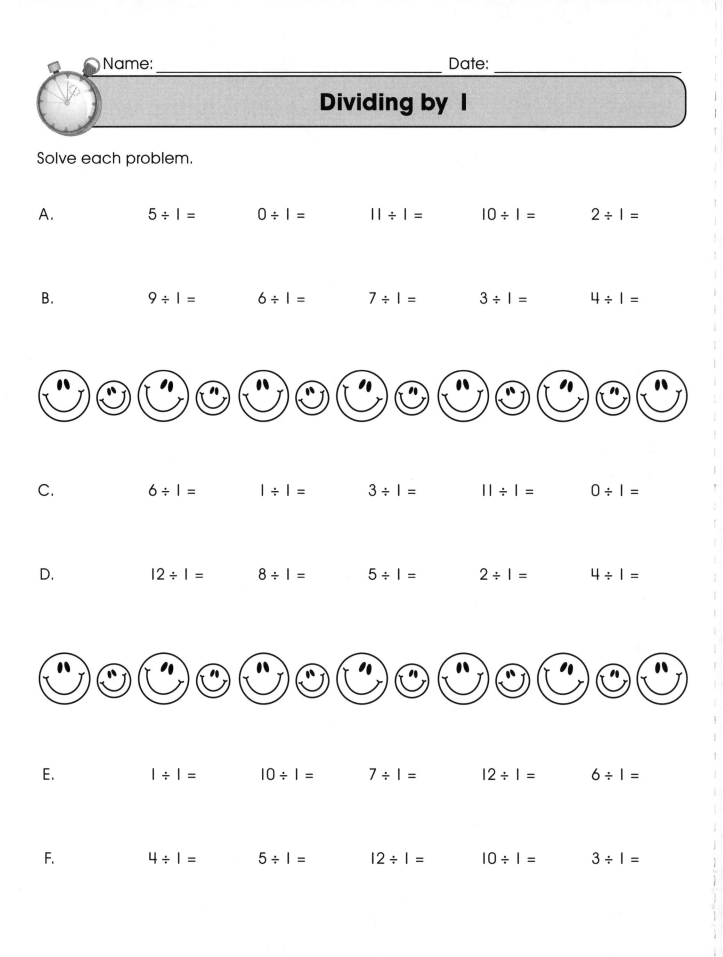

C.   6 ÷ 1 =   1 ÷ 1 =   3 ÷ 1 =   11 ÷ 1 =   0 ÷ 1 =

D.   12 ÷ 1 =   8 ÷ 1 =   5 ÷ 1 =   2 ÷ 1 =   4 ÷ 1 =

E.   1 ÷ 1 =   10 ÷ 1 =   7 ÷ 1 =   12 ÷ 1 =   6 ÷ 1 =

F.   4 ÷ 1 =   5 ÷ 1 =   12 ÷ 1 =   10 ÷ 1 =   3 ÷ 1 =

Dividing by 11

1 2 3 4 5
Minutes

A. $11 \div 11 =$ $11\overline{)44}$ $33 \div 11 =$ $11\overline{)99}$ $55 \div 11 =$

$11\overline{)88}$ $66 \div 11 =$ $11\overline{)0}$ $77 \div 11 =$ $11\overline{)11}$

B. $0 \div 11 =$ $11\overline{)33}$ $99 \div 11 =$ $11\overline{)55}$ $121 \div 11 =$

$11\overline{)66}$ $88 \div 11 =$ $11\overline{)110}$ $44 \div 11 =$ $11\overline{)132}$

- -

C. $44 \div 11 =$ $11\overline{)121}$ $22 \div 11 =$ $11\overline{)77}$ $33 \div 11 =$

$11\overline{)0}$ $66 \div 11 =$ $11\overline{)55}$ $110 \div 11 =$ $11\overline{)22}$

D. $88 \div 11 =$ $11\overline{)110}$ $132 \div 11 =$ $11\overline{)11}$ $121 \div 11 =$

$11\overline{)33}$ $0 \div 11 =$ $11\overline{)22}$ $99 \div 11 =$ $11\overline{)44}$

- -

E. $55 \div 11 =$ $11\overline{)88}$ $66 \div 11 =$ $11\overline{)0}$ $11 \div 11 =$

$11\overline{)66}$ $33 \div 11 =$ $11\overline{)22}$ $110 \div 11 =$ $11\overline{)132}$

F. $132 \div 11 =$ $11\overline{)22}$ $121 \div 11 =$ $11\overline{)110}$ $0 \div 11 =$

$11\overline{)77}$ $88 \div 11 =$ $11\overline{)44}$ $77 \div 11 =$ $11\overline{)121}$

Dividing by 11

Solve each problem. Circle the largest quotient to find which car wins the race.

A.

$33 \div 11 =$ $77 \div 11 =$ $11 \div 11 =$ $11\overline{)22}$

B.

$11\overline{)66}$ $11\overline{)99}$ $44 \div 11 =$ $0 \div 11 =$

C.

$88 \div 11 =$ $121 \div 11 =$ $44 \div 11 =$ $22 \div 11 =$

D.

$11\overline{)88}$ $11\overline{)121}$ $11\overline{)0}$ $11\overline{)110}$

E.

$33 \div 11 =$ $55 \div 11 =$ $66 \div 11 =$ $132 \div 11 =$

F.

$11\overline{)55}$ $11\overline{)33}$ $121 \div 11 =$ $11\overline{)44}$

Dividing by 12

A. $48 \div 12 =$ $12\overline{)24}$ $36 \div 12 =$ $12\overline{)60}$ $84 \div 12 =$

$12\overline{)96}$ $132 \div 12 =$ $12\overline{)72}$ $96 \div 12 =$ $12\overline{)108}$

B. $12 \div 12 =$ $12\overline{)120}$ $0 \div 12 =$ $12\overline{)132}$ $120 \div 12 =$

$12\overline{)0}$ $60 \div 12 =$ $12\overline{)48}$ $72 \div 12 =$ $12\overline{)12}$

C. $132 \div 12 =$ $12\overline{)48}$ $120 \div 12 =$ $12\overline{)108}$ $24 \div 12 =$

$12\overline{)144}$ $108 \div 12 =$ $12\overline{)24}$ $84 \div 12 =$ $12\overline{)36}$

D. $12 \div 12 =$ $12\overline{)84}$ $48 \div 12 =$ $12\overline{)60}$ $36 \div 12 =$

$12\overline{)120}$ $144 \div 12 =$ $12\overline{)12}$ $72 \div 12 =$ $12\overline{)132}$

E. $108 \div 12 =$ $12\overline{)36}$ $60 \div 12 =$ $12\overline{)144}$ $0 \div 12 =$

$12\overline{)72}$ $96 \div 12 =$ $12\overline{)108}$ $36 \div 12 =$ $12\overline{)0}$

F. $24 \div 12 =$ $12\overline{)60}$ $132 \div 12 =$ $12\overline{)120}$ $48 \div 12 =$

$12\overline{)96}$ $12 \div 12 =$ $12\overline{)24}$ $144 \div 12 =$ $12\overline{)48}$

Dividing by 12

Solve each problem.

A.

$84 \div 12 =$

$12\overline{)60}$

$72 \div 12 =$

$144 \div 12 =$

$12\overline{)36}$

B.

$12\overline{)120}$

$12\overline{)96}$

$24 \div 12 =$

$0 \div 12 =$

$48 \div 12 =$

C.

$96 \div 12 =$

$120 \div 12 =$

$132 \div 12 =$

$12 \div 12 =$

$12\overline{)144}$

D.

$12\overline{)60}$

$108 \div 12 =$

$144 \div 12 =$

$12\overline{)0}$

$48 \div 12 =$

E.

$72 \div 12 =$

$12\overline{)36}$

$12\overline{)24}$

$12 \div 12 =$

$84 \div 12 =$

Dividing by 10, 11, and 12

1 2 3 4 5 Minutes

A. $44 \div 11 =$ $12\overline{)24}$ $50 \div 10 =$ $11\overline{)132}$ $84 \div 12 =$

$10\overline{)40}$ $0 \div 11 =$ $12\overline{)144}$ $100 \div 10 =$ $11\overline{)77}$

B. $144 \div 12 =$ $10\overline{)120}$ $33 \div 11 =$ $11\overline{)99}$ $80 \div 10 =$

$11\overline{)11}$ $72 \div 12 =$ $10\overline{)0}$ $11 \div 11 =$ $12\overline{)132}$

C. $40 \div 10 =$ $10\overline{)70}$ $108 \div 12 =$ $11\overline{)22}$ $110 \div 11 =$

$12\overline{)24}$ $110 \div 10 =$ $10\overline{)50}$ $120 \div 12 =$ $11\overline{)44}$

D. $0 \div 11 =$ $10\overline{)80}$ $0 \div 12 =$ $11\overline{)11}$ $20 \div 10 =$

$11\overline{)33}$ $100 \div 10 =$ $12\overline{)132}$ $77 \div 11 =$ $12\overline{)144}$

E. $10 \div 10 =$ $10\overline{)0}$ $108 \div 12 =$ $11\overline{)0}$ $36 \div 12 =$

$11\overline{)55}$ $77 \div 11 =$ $10\overline{)40}$ $99 \div 11 =$ $12\overline{)84}$

F. $60 \div 10 =$ $10\overline{)50}$ $12 \div 12 =$ $10\overline{)10}$ $30 \div 10 =$

$11\overline{)88}$ $66 \div 11 =$ $12\overline{)120}$ $121 \div 11 =$ $12\overline{)60}$

A. $99 \div 11 =$ $12\overline{)132}$ $108 \div 12 =$ $10\overline{)0}$ $120 \div 10 =$

B. $10\overline{)110}$ $100 \div 10 =$ $11\overline{)55}$ $22 \div 11 =$ $12\overline{)84}$

C. $90 \div 10 =$ $11\overline{)88}$ $0 \div 11 =$ $12\overline{)120}$ $24 \div 12 =$

D. $10\overline{)60}$ $12 \div 12 =$ $11\overline{)77}$ $132 \div 11 =$ $12\overline{)72}$

E. $70 \div 10 =$ $11\overline{)110}$ $10 \div 10 =$ $10\overline{)50}$ $108 \div 12 =$

F. $10\overline{)30}$ $48 \div 12 =$ $11\overline{)99}$ $11 \div 11 =$ $11\overline{)121}$

Score

Cumulative Review: 0

A. $10\overline{)0}$ $7\overline{)0}$ $3\overline{)0}$ $12\overline{)0}$ $6\overline{)0}$ $5\overline{)0}$

B. $0 \times 3 =$ $4 \times 0 =$ $0 \times 6 =$ $12 \times 0 =$ $0 \times 11 =$ $0 \times 1 =$

C. $0 \div 1 =$ $0 \div 12 =$ $0 \div 4 =$ $0 \div 10 =$ $0 \div 5 =$ $0 \div 7 =$

D.
$$\begin{array}{r} 2 \\ \times\,0 \\ \hline \end{array} \quad \begin{array}{r} 10 \\ \times\,0 \\ \hline \end{array} \quad \begin{array}{r} 7 \\ \times\,0 \\ \hline \end{array} \quad \begin{array}{r} 0 \\ \times\,5 \\ \hline \end{array} \quad \begin{array}{r} 0 \\ \times\,0 \\ \hline \end{array} \quad \begin{array}{r} 0 \\ \times\,8 \\ \hline \end{array}$$

- -

E. $1\overline{)0}$ $4\overline{)0}$ $11\overline{)0}$ $10\overline{)0}$ $3\overline{)0}$ $2\overline{)0}$

F. $10 \times 0 =$ $3 \times 0 =$ $0 \times 8 =$ $9 \times 0 =$ $0 \times 0 =$ $0 \times 12 =$

G. $0 \div 11 =$ $0 \div 5 =$ $0 \div 2 =$ $0 \div 7 =$ $0 \div 3 =$ $0 \div 8 =$

H.
$$\begin{array}{r} 11 \\ \times\,0 \\ \hline \end{array} \quad \begin{array}{r} 0 \\ \times\,3 \\ \hline \end{array} \quad \begin{array}{r} 12 \\ \times\,0 \\ \hline \end{array} \quad \begin{array}{r} 0 \\ \times\,6 \\ \hline \end{array} \quad \begin{array}{r} 0 \\ \times\,4 \\ \hline \end{array} \quad \begin{array}{r} 0 \\ \times\,1 \\ \hline \end{array}$$

- -

I. $8\overline{)0}$ $6\overline{)0}$ $1\overline{)0}$ $9\overline{)0}$ $2\overline{)0}$ $7\overline{)0}$

J. $0 \times 7 =$ $11 \times 0 =$ $0 \times 2 =$ $0 \times 5 =$ $0 \times 10 =$ $0 \times 4 =$

K. $0 \div 6 =$ $0 \div 9 =$ $0 \div 10 =$ $0 \div 11 =$ $0 \div 1 =$ $0 \div 4 =$

L.
$$\begin{array}{r} 3 \\ \times\,0 \\ \hline \end{array} \quad \begin{array}{r} 9 \\ \times\,0 \\ \hline \end{array} \quad \begin{array}{r} 5 \\ \times\,0 \\ \hline \end{array} \quad \begin{array}{r} 6 \\ \times\,0 \\ \hline \end{array} \quad \begin{array}{r} 8 \\ \times\,0 \\ \hline \end{array} \quad \begin{array}{r} 0 \\ \times\,7 \\ \hline \end{array}$$

A. $1\overline{)1}$ $1\overline{)6}$ $1\overline{)7}$ $1\overline{)9}$ $1\overline{)11}$ $1\overline{)3}$

B. $1 \times 4 =$ $5 \times 1 =$ $1 \times 9 =$ $1 \times 2 =$ $1 \times 11 =$ $1 \times 0 =$

C. $0 \div 1 =$ $6 \div 1 =$ $5 \div 1 =$ $8 \div 1 =$ $2 \div 1 =$ $12 \div 1 =$

D.
$\begin{array}{r} 1 \\ \times\, 0 \\ \hline \end{array}$ $\begin{array}{r} 9 \\ \times\, 1 \\ \hline \end{array}$ $\begin{array}{r} 1 \\ \times\, 7 \\ \hline \end{array}$ $\begin{array}{r} 1 \\ \times\, 4 \\ \hline \end{array}$ $\begin{array}{r} 1 \\ \times\, 1 \\ \hline \end{array}$ $\begin{array}{r} 3 \\ \times\, 1 \\ \hline \end{array}$

E. $1\overline{)4}$ $1\overline{)2}$ $1\overline{)12}$ $1\overline{)5}$ $1\overline{)10}$ $1\overline{)8}$

F. $3 \times 1 =$ $1 \times 1 =$ $7 \times 1 =$ $1 \times 8 =$ $1 \times 6 =$ $9 \times 1 =$

G. $10 \div 1 =$ $12 \div 1 =$ $9 \div 1 =$ $7 \div 1 =$ $5 \div 1 =$ $4 \div 1 =$

H.
$\begin{array}{r} 1 \\ \times\, 2 \\ \hline \end{array}$ $\begin{array}{r} 11 \\ \times\, 1 \\ \hline \end{array}$ $\begin{array}{r} 1 \\ \times\, 8 \\ \hline \end{array}$ $\begin{array}{r} 1 \\ \times\, 5 \\ \hline \end{array}$ $\begin{array}{r} 12 \\ \times\, 1 \\ \hline \end{array}$ $\begin{array}{r} 10 \\ \times\, 1 \\ \hline \end{array}$

I. $1\overline{)12}$ $1\overline{)3}$ $1\overline{)0}$ $1\overline{)6}$ $1\overline{)10}$ $1\overline{)8}$

J. $1 \times 7 =$ $10 \times 1 =$ $2 \times 1 =$ $1 \times 3 =$ $12 \times 1 =$ $4 \times 1 =$

K. $3 \div 1 =$ $1 \div 1 =$ $6 \div 1 =$ $9 \div 1 =$ $11 \div 1 =$ $3 \div 1 =$

L.
$\begin{array}{r} 6 \\ \times\, 1 \\ \hline \end{array}$ $\begin{array}{r} 1 \\ \times\, 3 \\ \hline \end{array}$ $\begin{array}{r} 10 \\ \times\, 1 \\ \hline \end{array}$ $\begin{array}{r} 2 \\ \times\, 1 \\ \hline \end{array}$ $\begin{array}{r} 4 \\ \times\, 1 \\ \hline \end{array}$ $\begin{array}{r} 7 \\ \times\, 1 \\ \hline \end{array}$

Answer Key

PAGE 26
A. 3; B. 6; C. 18; D. 36; E. 27;
F. 21; G. 15; H. 30; I. 33; J. 0;
K. 9; L. 12

PAGE 27
A. 6, 18, 0, 6, 12, 18, 24, 0, 12,
30; B. 42, 54, 36, 48, 60, 42,
30, 72, 24, 48; C. 66, 54, 0, 12,
60, 12, 6, 0, 72, 18; D. 24, 30,
42, 54, 48, 36, 30, 6, 18, 48;
E. 66, 42, 54, 24, 0, 18, 12, 36,
6, 66; F. 54, 24, 48, 30, 72, 0,
12, 30, 42, 60

PAGE 28
A. 0, 30, 24, 6, 48; B. 36, 6, 18,
24, 54; C. 72, 12, 42, 60, 48;
D. 54, 12, 0, 18, 30; E. 42, 36,
24, 66, 18; F. 66, 72, 30, 48, 54

PAGE 29
A. 9, 0, 27, 36, 0, 54, 9, 18, 45,
54; B. 36, 18, 63, 90, 72, 99, 27,
72, 63, 81; C. 54, 108, 0, 36,
81, 9, 63, 45, 54, 18; D. 63, 45,
90, 27, 0, 36, 18, 72, 108, 27;
E. 54, 99, 72, 108, 0, 45, 63, 18,
9, 36; F. 27, 45, 9, 36, 54, 81, 27,
63, 90, 72

PAGE 30
A. 54, 45, 18, 72; B. 0, 108, 63,
36; C. 99, 81, 0, 108; D. 63, 90,
18, 36; E. 27, 45, 9, 63; F. 18, 90,
72, 99; G. 81, 27, 54, 9

PAGE 31
A. 0, 12, 9, 42, 24, 36, 18, 0, 18,
66; B. 0, 36, 18, 6, 6, 72, 33,
15, 27, 12; C. 30, 9, 24, 45, 48,
81, 3, 99, 24, 30; D. 0, 27, 54,
21, 72, 42, 18, 54, 36, 108;
E. 72, 3, 0, 63, 36, 30, 21, 6, 0,
12; F. 24, 15, 90, 45, 63, 48, 60,
6, 9, 6

PAGE 32
A. 0, 18, 18, 54, 6; B. 15, 60, 48,
12, 108; C. 30, 21, 30, 3, 24;
D. 0, 27, 63, 9, 33; E. 27, 36, 9,
81, 48; F. 72, 72, 36, 99, 36

PAGE 33
A. 0, 5, 18, 6, 10, 9, 7, 30, 24,
11; B. 14, 45, 5, 0, 21, 120, 10,
40, 21, 110; C. 14, 0, 40, 66,
24, 0, 81, 30, 72, 42; D. 36, 15,
33, 42, 60, 0, 36, 6, 12, 35;
E. 48, 55, 100, 0, 63, 1, 63, 27,
48, 22; F. 4, 72, 108, 25, 0, 54,
72, 12, 18, 35

PAGE 34
A. 10, 35, 3, 8, 9, 0, 8, 11, 0, 18;
B. 16, 63, 9, 35, 45, 15, 42, 48,
18, 120; C. 54, 22, 21, 40, 55,
20, 2, 63, 12, 0; D. 24, 24,
24, 10, 108, 8, 9, 30, 10, 33;
E. 45, 110, 81, 16, 100, 24, 21,
42, 48, 60; F. 54, 72, 2, 8, 36,
20, 0, 120, 10, 0

PAGE 35
A. 32, 36, 16, 12, 36, 4, 24, 40,
48, 24; B. 8, 4, 0, 40, 20, 8, 12,
28, 32, 44; C. 20, 4, 16, 12, 16,
4, 28, 48, 24, 8; D. 0, 48, 20, 8,
12, 32, 28, 44, 36, 0; E. 24, 44,
4, 32, 8, 36, 44, 4, 0, 48; F. 16,
20, 32, 0, 24, 36, 12, 28, 40, 16

PAGE 36
A. 4, 8, 24, 20, 36, 28, 48;
B. 40, 44, 8, 20, 28, 12, 24;
C. 32, 20, 0, 36, 24, 32, 4;
D. 8, 16, 12, 44, 28, 24, 20;
E. 40, 32, 16, 0, 8, 20, 36;
F. 44, 28, 0, 12, 8, 40, 24;
Car A wins.

PAGE 37
A. 0, 48, 0, 64, 24, 72, 96, 40,
16, 8; B. 24, 32, 40, 80, 32, 16,
88, 56, 72, 56; C. 0, 48, 32, 64,
0, 96, 56, 16, 56, 64; D. 72, 80,
24, 16, 32, 48, 88, 8, 40, 24;
E. 72, 40, 48, 0, 96, 80, 72, 48,
64, 88; F. 16, 32, 8, 24, 40, 0,
64, 56, 16, 24

PAGE 38
A. 0, 96, 48, 88, 72, 16;
B. 56, 64, 40, 32, 24, 32;
C. 16, 8, 72, 48, 40, 80;
D. 0, 24, 56, 88, 40, 64

PAGE 39
A. 14, 0, 7, 21, 35, 84, 28, 21,
7, 56; B. 77, 28, 35, 0, 63, 70,
63, 42, 49, 56; C. 42, 49, 0, 63,
84, 7, 14, 63, 35, 21; D. 28, 77,
35, 56, 0, 70, 42, 21, 14, 7;
E. 56, 49, 28, 56, 84, 0, 42, 70,
42, 77; F. 21, 63, 49, 14, 35, 7,
0, 7, 28, 14

PAGE 40
A. 0; B. 28; C. 42; D. 7; E. 21;
F. 70; G. 63; H. 14; I. 21; J. 56;
K. 63; L. 49; M. 35; N. 77; O. 42;
P. 84; Q. 0; R. 35; S. 77; T. 28;
U. 84; V. 14; W. 7; X. 56

PAGE 41
A. 80, 0, 35, 4, 8, 48, 8, 28, 56,
42; B. 32, 0, 32, 72, 16, 12, 20,
88, 0, 77; C. 84, 64, 72, 44,
20, 80, 16, 7, 48, 49; D. 70, 40,
40, 48, 16, 56, 0, 96, 40, 21;
E. 35, 16, 4, 0, 48, 24, 14, 32,
49, 7; F. 44, 24, 28, 0, 36, 20,
88, 80, 8, 84

Answer Key

PAGE 42
A. 20, 70, 24, 80, 35; B. 48, 0, 40, 0, 96; C. 42, 8, 72, 40, 77; D. 8, 14, 32, 24, 28; E. 64, 44, 16, 7, 36; F. 49, 88, 12, 48, 4

PAGE 43
A. 0, 0, 14, 8, 90, 60, 18, 40, 24, 80; B. 63, 66, 36, 48, 84, 8, 100, 25, 0, 35; C. 0, 11, 22, 28, 0, 24, 30, 36, 49, 9; D. 5, 15, 40, 0, 45, 120, 12, 0, 24, 50; E. 3, 110, 30, 20, 42, 24, 6, 4, 1, 60; F. 99, 56, 0, 20, 10, 16, 96, 0, 44, 6

PAGE 44
A. 12, 60, 0, 63, 10, 9, 16, 50, 35, 3; B. 72, 48, 100, 60, 120, 0, 18, 10, 84, 33; C. 42, 0, 14, 27, 12, 84, 12, 32, 63, 6; D. 18, 36, 21, 72, 72, 7, 27, 48, 40, 40; E. 36, 4, 56, 25, 48, 18, 96, 77, 20, 28; F. 54, 64, 80, 33, 7, 25, 24, 16, 35, 10

PAGE 45
A. 66, 55, 0, 44, 22, 66, 33, 44, 77, 11; B. 77, 99, 22, 55, 88, 0, 11, 88, 99, 33; C. 77, 11, 33, 66, 99, 66, 22, 77, 0, 132; D. 88, 110, 55, 88, 121, 0, 55, 132, 121, 44; E. 66, 110, 11, 110, 99, 33, 22, 33, 11, 77; F. 44, 132, 88, 55, 22, 132, 0, 121, 77, 44

PAGE 46
A. 99, 0, 22, 44, 77, 33, 88; B. 22, 121, 33, 44, 66, 110, 55; C. 11, 77, 99, 0, 22, 88, 132; D. 66, 88, 22, 44, 99, 110, 11; E. 0, 55, 110, 66, 33, 44, 77; F. 121, 22, 99, 110, 11, 66, 44; Ship C arrives first.

PAGE 47
A. 120, 36, 120, 0, 60, 108, 144, 96, 24, 48; B. 48, 60, 24, 12, 132, 84, 96, 108, 72, 132; C. 60, 24, 36, 96, 0, 108, 132, 84, 72, 0; D. 72, 12, 48, 144, 60, 84, 132, 12, 24, 108; E. 144, 0, 12, 132, 36, 12, 72, 84, 36, 96; F. 108, 84, 132, 60, 72, 0, 48, 120, 24, 144

PAGE 48
A. 24, 36, 84, 12, 108; B. 72, 60, 96, 12, 144; C. 120, 24, 72, 48, 36; D. 84, 48, 108, 144, 120; E. 60, 132, 96, 84, 24

PAGE 49
A. 77, 24, 55, 0, 108, 110, 144, 33, 0, 72; B. 22, 88, 60, 36, 44, 11, 12, 84, 132, 120; C. 66, 99, 96, 36, 48, 96, 33, 121, 0, 22; D. 77, 108, 144, 110, 88, 55, 12, 84, 120, 132; E. 99, 72, 96, 60, 24, 66, 44, 48, 120, 55; F. 110, 24, 132, 11, 121, 0, 48, 88, 12, 77

PAGE 50
A. 72, 132, 77, 66, 108; B. 96, 72, 33, 84, 110; C. 121, 96, 77, 120, 108; D. 44, 12, 110, 0, 24; E. 60, 11, 55, 72, 36; F. 22, 48, 88, 132, 99

PAGE 51
A. 42, 25, 12, 36, 18, 28, 96, 22, 48, 81; B. 0, 6, 11, 0, 18, 9, 3, 72, 36, 0; C. 2, 5, 40, 9, 30, 50, 56, 32, 40, 0; D. 0, 20, 55, 0, 8, 72, 60, 70, 16, 0; E. 24, 20, 10, 27, 36, 16, 0, 110, 64, 0; F. 0, 30, 0, 63, 33, 12, 0, 12, 77, 80

PAGE 52
A. 0, 8, 14, 0, 1, 14, 20, 7, 4, 0; B. 0, 16, 6, 11, 0, 4, 6, 0, 3, 18; C. 0, 5, 8, 4, 16, 0, 8, 0, 12, 5; D. 24, 0, 2, 10, 0, 9, 4, 2, 6, 12; E. 12, 2, 10, 0, 8, 0, 12, 22, 0, 10; F. 0, 0, 0, 11, 3, 18, 9, 7, 44, 6

PAGE 53
A. 28, 35, 21, 48, 18, 50, 45, 36, 24, 10; B. 33, 0, 20, 32, 6, 60, 0, 36, 30, 20; C. 32, 5, 28, 6, 55, 36, 44, 15, 40, 24; D. 9, 16, 0, 12, 48, 35, 3, 60, 24, 0; E. 40, 35, 9, 55, 10, 40, 15, 30, 25, 60; F. 0, 8, 44, 4, 27, 16, 35, 36, 8, 0

PAGE 54
A. 16, 25, 18, 0, 3, 60, 0, 5, 0, 35; B. 48, 12, 20, 15, 30, 40, 8, 40, 22, 0; C. 44, 1, 8, 6, 2, 36, 24, 16, 0, 27; D. 0, 7, 18, 10, 9, 14, 12, 0, 4, 15; E. 0, 32, 12, 33, 16, 27, 0, 11, 35, 36; F. 30, 28, 9, 0, 50, 0, 4, 4, 45, 10

PAGE 55
A. 72, 24, 77, 56, 6, 88, 0, 40, 21, 54; B. 18, 24, 96, 8, 60, 66, 0, 48, 84, 16; C. 60, 70, 49, 8, 54, 32, 35, 6, 66, 21; D. 72, 14, 36, 28, 63, 64, 42, 0, 96, 56; E. 30, 36, 8, 64, 0, 35, 77, 18, 40, 24; F. 56, 24, 12, 7, 16, 6, 88, 0, 63, 48

PAGE 56
A. 0, 108, 45, 0, 33, 27, 70, 9, 36, 18; B. 81, 0, 60, 44, 121, 10, 72, 84, 80, 72; C. 11, 120, 48, 20, 66, 96, 84, 60, 36, 70; D. 40, 144, 50, 63, 30, 22, 24, 99, 0, 12; E. 90, 121, 110, 9, 44, 77, 30, 45, 0, 66; F. 54, 96, 55, 88, 27, 100, 108, 132, 50, 81

PAGE 57
A. 0, 63, 21, 88, 90, 9, 45, 36, 0, 96; B. 55, 24, 60, 66, 48, 24, 42, 121, 10, 72; C. 56, 88, 30, 70, 49, 72, 18, 12, 72, 54; D. 50, 40, 36, 77, 80, 18, 20, 132, 12, 44; E. 8, 11, 63, 99, 84, 96, 22, 32, 14, 108; F. 84, 144, 35, 110, 72, 120, 54, 0, 30, 70

PAGE 58
A. 49, 24, 0, 60, 24, 50, 3, 64, 84, 36; B. 55, 4, 10, 10, 36, 15, 8, 12, 7, 16; C. 25, 28, 20, 77, 18, 0, 84, 5, 0, 24; D. 48, 32, 121, 0, 20, 0, 88, 0, 63, 7; E. 6, 144, 0, 44, 1, 110, 9, 45, 30, 108; F. 12, 54, 40, 55, 0, 81, 48, 45, 10, 0

PAGE 59
A. 0, 5, 50, 72, 24, 10, 22, 44, 90, 0; B. 66, 0, 24, 6, 88, 24, 12, 4, 120, 56; C. 42, 32, 9, 14, 28, 96, 0, 63, 100, 36; D. 36, 40, 0, 54, 20, 120, 11, 0, 48, 72; E. 12, 110, 16, 16, 0, 20, 77, 90, 0, 2; F. 0, 50, 72, 33, 0, 96, 28, 9, 15, 0

PAGE 60
A. 64, 18, 30, 55, 21, 72, 90, 7, 35, 36; B. 72, 28, 6, 0, 60, 18, 56, 11, 10, 48; C. 40, 27, 54, 32, 28, 144, 0, 81, 15, 14; D. 56, 20, 16, 18, 77, 132, 30, 99, 110, 35; E. 12, 12, 54, 28, 60, 44, 72, 84, 49, 108; F. 4, 30, 18, 4, 0, 21, 55, 80, 72, 48

PAGE 61
A. 96, 121, 72, 60, 77, 81, 132, 40, 72, 54; B. 63, 120, 48, 144, 27, 110, 108, 55, 0, 44; C. 24, 60, 33, 18, 36, 72, 70, 66, 0, 64; D. 28, 24, 132, 84, 30, 99, 14, 40, 36, 10; E. 32, 80, 45, 49, 90, 0, 12, 16, 48, 8; F. 36, 7, 24, 27, 72, 25, 16, 40, 63, 60

PAGE 62
A. 0, 16, 21, 24, 144, 30, 72, 70, 84, 60; B. 12, 0, 40, 48, 56, 18, 66, 36, 110, 33; C. 72, 9, 70, 2, 15, 18, 60, 6, 84, 55; D. 72, 100, 28, 42, 24, 77, 27, 10, 45, 30; E. 60, 0, 2, 35, 21, 12, 24, 88, 40, 42; F. 25, 48, 120, 32, 49, 36, 24, 6, 42, 30

PAGE 63
A. 9, 4, 0, 12, 7, 5, 6, 3, 11, 1; B. 2, 8, 10, 6, 4, 0, 5, 11, 1, 6; C. 7, 10, 4, 7, 12, 2, 5, 0, 8, 2; D. 9, 4, 2, 12, 3, 7, 0, 1, 11, 3; E. 2, 8, 10, 5, 0, 6, 7, 3, 9, 4; F. 3, 11, 1, 9, 6, 0, 4, 10, 12, 2

PAGE 64
A. 5, 0, 11, 10, 2; B. 9, 6, 7, 3, 4; C. 6, 1, 3, 11, 0; D. 12, 8, 5, 2, 4; E. 1, 10, 7, 12, 6; F. 4, 5, 12, 10, 3

PAGE 65
A. 11, 0, 6, 1, 3, 12, 7, 9, 5, 8; B. 0, 10, 8, 6, 1, 11, 4, 7, 9, 5; C. 10, 2, 0, 3, 2, 4, 7, 8, 11, 7; D. 9, 1, 12, 0, 1, 5, 3, 10, 4, 6; E. 6, 3, 2, 7, 8, 12, 3, 9, 5, 10; F. 1, 8, 4, 2, 11, 11, 9, 5, 7, 1

PAGE 66
A. 11; B. 8; C. 4; D. 9; E. 7; F. 12; G. 3; H. 5; I. 1; J. 6

PAGE 67
A. 2, 4, 0, 8, 6, 0, 5, 6, 3, 7; B. 10, 12, 9, 2, 12, 5, 11, 10, 4, 11; C. 4, 7, 0, 4, 8, 3, 6, 10, 11, 1; D. 1, 9, 3, 5, 9, 0, 8, 11, 7, 8; E. 4, 11, 10, 12, 2, 0, 7, 4, 8, 5; F. 5, 8, 11, 7, 1, 2, 12, 1, 0, 9

PAGE 68
A. 6, 10, 8, 11; B. 3, 5, 12, 2; C. 9, 0, 7, 4; D. 8, 12, 7, 6; E. 11, 8, 10, 5

PAGE 69
A. 2, 4, 1, 12, 0, 4, 12, 10, 9, 8; B. 9, 0, 12, 12, 6, 5, 2, 7, 11, 4; C. 8, 1, 5, 0, 3, 1, 0, 9, 3, 6; D. 10, 2, 9, 4, 1, 6, 3, 5, 5, 7; E. 12, 0, 4, 9, 0, 6, 1, 1, 4, 8; F. 2, 8, 9, 4, 1, 3, 8, 5, 7, 3

PAGE 70
A. 4, 1, 12, 11, 9; B. 1, 2, 5, 6, 7; C. 6, 7, 8, 12, 12; D. 0, 6, 5, 10, 11; E. 9, 3, 0, 11, 3; F. 5, 1, 8, 4, 3

PAGE 71
A. 4, 2, 3, 0, 7, 0, 5, 10, 2, 4; B. 0, 12, 8, 6, 12, 5, 10, 9, 6, 8; C. 8, 12, 9, 3, 6, 1, 4, 11, 10, 9; D. 3, 7, 12, 8, 5, 6, 1, 5, 11, 0; E. 6, 3, 2, 12, 1, 7, 5, 10, 3, 5; F. 8, 6, 7, 4, 0, 1, 12, 0, 10, 8

PAGE 72
A. 4, 7, 12, 5; B. 0, 1, 4, 8; C. 3, 6, 1, 2; D. 12, 11, 7, 8; E. 11, 3, 9, 5; F. 4, 0, 2, 10; G. 2, 9, 8, 12

PAGE 73
A. 11, 5, 4, 12, 7, 0, 8, 9, 6, 2; B. 3, 7, 2, 11, 1, 3, 5, 8, 9, 10; C. 7, 2, 6, 10, 5, 6, 0, 1, 12, 11; D. 2, 5, 3, 4, 9, 12, 8, 7, 4, 8; E. 6, 4, 7, 12, 5, 5, 2, 0, 8, 9; F. 11, 8, 9, 6, 0, 7, 12, 11, 4, 2

Answer Key

PAGE 74
A. 5, 0, 8, 11; B. 2, 4, 10, 6;
C. 4, 10, 3, 12; D. 11, 3, 0, 9;
E. 5, 1, 6, 11; F. 5, 4, 7, 8; Shark
C wins.

PAGE 75
A. 1, 10, 9, 0, 7, 9, 4, 3, 12, 4;
B. 3, 12, 6, 1, 0, 6, 10, 7, 1, 5;
C. 10, 0, 5, 2, 8, 4, 0, 8, 6, 7;
D. 2, 10, 12, 11, 3, 3, 11, 6, 4, 5;
E. 3, 4, 5, 8, 11, 9, 2, 0, 10, 7;
F. 4, 3, 6, 2, 1, 11, 8, 5, 9, 1

PAGE 76
A. 4, 6, 0, 3; B. 2, 8, 12, 10;
C. 5, 1, 6, 9; D. 2, 11, 9, 6;
E. 11, 8, 5, 4; F. 12, 10, 0, 7

PAGE 77
A. 5, 7, 5, 4, 2, 1, 1, 1, 11, 12;
B. 12, 7, 4, 9, 2, 0, 11, 0, 2, 2;
C. 4, 8, 4, 6, 0, 11, 8, 11, 3, 5;
D. 10, 12, 4, 8, 7, 10, 2, 12, 12,
5; E. 6, 1, 0, 7, 4, 9, 11, 11, 3, 9;
F. 5, 11, 1, 4, 2, 2, 7, 11, 9, 0

PAGE 78
A. 7, 2, 1, 4, 11; B. 6, 12, 3, 5, 4;
C. 10, 10, 2, 6, 9; D. 0, 9, 8, 8,
12; E. 0, 6, 7, 5, 8; F. 8, 12, 11,
10, 5

PAGE 79
A. 9, 3, 8, 11, 4, 0, 1, 9, 3, 2;
B. 0, 5, 4, 0, 1, 4, 11, 12, 2, 3;
C. 10, 5, 0, 4, 5, 7, 9, 5, 4, 1;
D. 11, 2, 1, 12, 9, 11, 3, 10, 7, 1;
E. 2, 4, 7, 4, 0, 6, 12, 1, 6, 8;
F. 12, 12, 3, 5, 8, 0, 12, 3, 10, 3

PAGE 80
A. 2, 8, 0, 11, 6, 12, 1, 2, 10, 6;
B. 8, 5, 3, 10, 9, 11, 8, 4, 4, 10;
C. 11, 0, 5, 7, 1, 8, 5, 6, 12, 8;
D. 9, 6, 2, 8, 5, 12, 4, 11, 12, 0;
E. 6, 4, 5, 8, 8, 8, 9, 3, 7, 7;
F. 10, 9, 8, 10, 9, 2, 9, 5, 10, 6

PAGE 81
A. 3, 6, 8, 3, 7, 12, 2, 11, 1, 8;
B. 4, 0, 5, 9, 0, 2, 11, 4, 12, 1;
C. 5, 7, 2, 8, 9, 10, 1, 3, 2, 12;
D. 6, 11, 1, 2, 10, 9, 4, 5, 11, 4;
E. 2, 0, 8, 12, 3, 5, 12, 9, 0, 2;
F. 11, 1, 5, 6, 4, 4, 7, 10, 0, 11

PAGE 82
A. 6; B. 12; C. 4; D. 0; E. 7; F. 1;
G. 9; H. 4; I. 7; J. 8; K. 5; L. 3;
M. 1; N. 12; O. 11; P. 10; Q. 2;
R. 0; S. 6; T. 8; U. 9; V. 5; W. 10;
X. 2

PAGE 83
A. 7, 1, 4, 5, 12, 4, 2, 11, 3, 2;
B. 8, 9, 6, 0, 5, 12, 11, 7, 0, 6;
C. 11, 2, 0, 8, 6, 4, 5, 9, 1, 7;
D. 9, 5, 10, 11, 2, 0, 7, 3, 4, 10;
E. 5, 4, 3, 6, 12, 2, 3, 8, 10, 7;
F. 7, 11, 9, 10, 8, 12, 6, 0, 1, 3

PAGE 84
A. 11; B. 2; C. 12; D. 3; E. 7; F. 6;
G. 0; H. 5; I. 9; J. 10; K. 8; L. 4

PAGE 85
A. 0, 12, 8, 3, 7, 9, 10, 7, 3, 4;
B. 1, 11, 5, 8, 12, 0, 11, 5, 9, 1;
C. 6, 8, 3, 9, 4, 6, 1, 11, 2, 10;
D. 7, 3, 10, 1, 11, 2, 0, 4, 8, 7;
E. 12, 1, 3, 9, 6, 8, 1, 12, 2, 11;
F. 0, 6, 4, 1, 5, 10, 11, 0, 8, 3

PAGE 86
A. 11, 1, 7, 3; B. 2, 4, 9, 0;
C. 3, 11, 10, 8; D. 4, 2, 12, 6;
E. 12, 7, 5, 8; F. 1, 6, 0, 9

PAGE 87
A. 1, 5, 2, 11, 12, 1, 9, 6, 6, 10;
B. 0, 9, 2, 4, 9, 2, 2, 0, 5, 0;
C. 1, 10, 6, 2, 12, 8, 10, 3, 8, 8;
D. 4, 5, 11, 10, 12, 1, 0, 6, 2, 9;
E. 8, 12, 6, 12, 0, 5, 8, 3, 10, 7;
F. 3, 11, 2, 7, 11, 0, 3, 9, 3, 3

PAGE 88
A. 5, 5, 8, 8, 10; B. 12, 7, 10, 12,
5; C. 8, 9, 12, 12, 7; D. 5, 9, 8,
7, 10; E. 9, 7, 11, 5, 5; F. 3, 3, 1,
6, 4

PAGE 89
A. 6, 12, 9, 3, 1, 9, 5, 0, 12, 10;
B. 4, 11, 3, 7, 11, 1, 10, 5, 2, 8;
C. 12, 10, 4, 5, 8, 6, 0, 3, 2, 7;
D. 10, 2, 1, 9, 6, 12, 5, 0, 9, 8;
E. 1, 0, 4, 2, 3, 11, 9, 12, 6, 1;
F. 0, 7, 2, 4, 7, 10, 12, 9, 8, 5

PAGE 90
A. 6, 12, 0, 8, 2; B. 0, 4, 10, 7, 3;
C. 0, 9, 11, 7, 12; D. 10, 11, 8, 5,
4; E. 12, 3, 1, 5, 2; F. 7, 6, 4, 9, 10

PAGE 91
A. 1, 4, 3, 9, 5, 8, 6, 0, 7, 1;
B. 0, 3, 9, 5, 11, 6, 8, 10, 4, 12;
C. 4, 11, 2, 7, 3, 0, 6, 5, 10, 2;
D. 8, 10, 12, 1, 11, 3, 0, 2, 9, 4;
E. 5, 8, 6, 0, 1, 6, 3, 2, 10, 12;
F. 12, 2, 11, 10, 0, 7, 8, 4, 7, 11

PAGE 92
A. 3, 7, 1, 2; B. 6, 9, 4, 0;
C. 8, 11, 4, 2; D. 8, 11, 0, 10;
E. 3, 5, 6, 12; F. 5, 3, 11, 4;
Car E wins.

Answer Key

PAGE 93
A. 4, 2, 3, 5, 7, 8, 11, 6, 8, 9;
B. 1, 10, 0, 11, 10, 0, 5, 4, 6, 1;
C. 11, 4, 10, 9, 2, 12, 9, 2, 7, 3;
D. 1, 7, 4, 5, 3, 10, 12, 1, 6, 11;
E. 9, 3, 5, 12, 0, 6, 8, 9, 3, 0;
F. 2, 5, 11, 10, 4, 8, 1, 2, 12, 4

PAGE 94
A. 7, 5, 6, 12, 3; B. 10, 8, 2, 0, 4;
C. 8, 10, 11, 1, 12; D. 5, 9, 12, 0,
4; E. 6, 3, 2, 1, 7

PAGE 95
A. 4, 2, 5, 12, 7, 4, 0, 12, 10, 7;
B. 12, 12, 3, 9, 8, 1, 6, 0, 1, 11;
C. 4, 7, 9, 2, 10, 2, 11, 5, 10, 4;
D. 0, 8, 0, 1, 2, 3, 10, 11, 7, 12;
E. 1, 0, 9, 0, 3, 5, 7, 4, 9, 7;
F. 6, 5, 1, 1, 3, 8, 6, 10, 11, 5

PAGE 96
A. 9, 11, 9, 0, 12; B. 11, 10, 5, 2,
7; C. 9, 8, 0, 10, 2; D. 6, 1, 7, 12,
6; E. 7, 10, 1, 5, 9; F. 3, 4, 9, 1, 11

PAGE 97
A. 9, 1, 4, 0, 3, 7, 6, 9, 2, 6;
B. 10, 2, 4, 4, 3, 6, 5, 4, 5, 3;
C. 11, 7, 8, 9, 7, 6, 12, 1, 4, 8;
D. 4, 8, 9, 0, 10, 3, 1, 5, 0, 3;
E. 0, 4, 2, 12, 4, 4, 12, 10, 9, 8;
F. 12, 0, 8, 12, 6, 10, 3, 7, 1, 4

PAGE 98
A. 9, 1, 0, 4, 1, 6, 11, 7, 3, 9;
B. 6, 11, 5, 11, 6, 3, 5, 6, 5, 0;
C. 9, 3, 5, 4, 2, 1, 1, 7, 12, 6;
D. 12, 7, 4, 9, 2, 0, 0, 10, 5, 1;
E. 5, 8, 4, 6, 0, 9, 7, 11, 12, 5;
F. 6, 12, 12, 8, 3, 12, 2, 12, 11, 5

PAGE 99
A. 7, 10, 6, 3, 6, 5, 11, 5, 8, 8;
B. 4, 2, 10, 1, 9, 1, 12, 9, 3, 5;
C. 11, 12, 6, 12, 7, 6, 8, 3, 11, 7;
D. 2, 11, 11, 7, 12, 8, 4, 2, 4, 6;
E. 9, 1, 2, 3, 12, 7, 9, 6, 6, 7;
F. 8, 9, 5, 4, 9, 4, 6, 8, 2, 1

PAGE 100
A. 12, 10, 4, 0, 9, 4, 1, 8, 7, 7;
B. 3, 5, 12, 1, 5, 11, 9, 5, 11, 4;
C. 7, 10, 8, 2, 6, 6, 11, 4, 10, 7;
D. 2, 12, 0, 2, 1, 6, 1, 0, 10, 6;
E. 2, 7, 8, 5, 12, 2, 11, 5, 3, 4;
F. 3, 11, 0, 1, 8, 9, 1, 7, 7, 10

PAGE 101
A. 6, 1, 12, 8, 0, 2, 9, 4, 12, 11;
B. 2, 5, 4, 10, 5, 9, 1, 7, 8, 9;
C. 4, 2, 0, 0, 12, 7, 7, 10, 11, 2;
D. 5, 9, 8, 11, 0, 12, 7, 12, 5, 6;
E. 5, 3, 3, 12, 11, 6, 6, 9, 7, 0;
F. 8, 10, 5, 9, 5, 1, 4, 5, 9, 2

PAGE 102
A. 8, 11, 0, 9, 4, 3, 10, 0, 2, 6;
B. 0, 6, 5, 4, 1, 5, 7, 5, 10, 7;
C. 5, 3, 0, 11, 6, 8, 12, 4, 10, 1;
D. 2, 3, 4, 0, 12, 10, 11, 9, 1, 5;
E. 9, 3, 1, 4, 2, 0, 9, 5, 6, 8;
F. 12, 4, 9, 2, 7, 8, 8, 12, 12, 7

PAGE 103
A. 4, 1, 11, 8, 5, 6, 11, 2, 6, 10;
B. 4, 4, 9, 8, 10, 12, 10, 1, 11, 2;
C. 8, 11, 5, 12, 12, 10, 7, 3, 5,
12; D. 7, 11, 0, 11, 9, 1, 4, 6, 6, 8;
E. 3, 4, 9, 2, 10, 9, 11, 6, 0, 1;
F. 5, 11, 7, 9, 7, 7, 4, 6, 5, 6

PAGE 104
A. 9, 7, 10, 9, 3, 2, 4, 9, 12, 7;
B. 7, 5, 4, 8, 5, 9, 5, 8, 3, 11;
C. 4, 8, 9, 5, 0, 5, 3, 9, 9, 10;
D. 11, 4, 6, 5, 11, 12, 11, 4, 4, 3;
E. 8, 8, 12, 6, 10, 2, 6, 11, 7, 6;
F. 11, 6, 3, 2, 9, 2, 7, 2, 1, 4

PAGE 105
A. 7, 11, 12, 4, 5, 9, 8, 12, 2, 8;
B. 4, 12, 3, 10, 12, 0, 9, 10, 7,
12; C. 4, 6, 2, 10, 9, 3, 12, 6, 4,
11; D. 9, 5, 5, 9, 8, 2, 4, 9, 6, 2;
E. 8, 6, 7, 2, 4, 7, 10, 8, 6, 7;
F. 2, 12, 7, 3, 8, 5, 11, 12, 5, 12

PAGE 106
A. 4, 8, 9, 6, 5, 10, 5, 4, 5, 5;
B. 11, 10, 8, 7, 4, 11, 6, 4, 2, 12;
C. 3, 5, 11, 8, 8, 8, 10, 9, 1, 10;
D. 9, 11, 8, 5, 2, 6, 9, 5, 8, 6;
E. 7, 11, 11, 4, 10, 2, 9, 12, 1, 9;
F. 4, 11, 1, 8, 2, 4, 7, 11, 10, 9

PAGE 107
A. 0, 0, 0, 0, 0, 0; B. 0, 0, 0, 0,
0, 0; C. 0, 0, 0, 0, 0, 0; D. 0, 0,
0, 0, 0, 0; E. 0, 0, 0, 0, 0, 0;
F. 0, 0, 0, 0, 0, 0; G. 0, 0, 0, 0,
0, 0; H. 0, 0, 0, 0, 0, 0; I. 0, 0, 0,
0, 0, 0; J. 0, 0, 0, 0, 0, 0; K. 0, 0,
0, 0, 0, 0; L. 0, 0, 0, 0, 0, 0

PAGE 108
A. 1, 6, 7, 9, 11, 3; B. 4, 5, 9, 2,
11, 0; C. 0, 6, 5, 8, 2, 12; D. 0, 9,
7, 4, 1, 3; E. 4, 2, 12, 5, 10, 8;
F. 3, 1, 7, 8, 6, 9; G. 10, 12, 9,
7, 5, 4; H. 2, 11, 8, 5, 12, 10;
I. 12, 3, 0, 6, 10, 8; J. 7, 10, 2, 3,
12, 4; K. 3, 1, 6, 9, 11, 3; L. 6, 3,
10, 2, 4, 7

PAGE 109
A. 4, 2, 6, 1, 9, 8; B. 14, 20, 4,
10, 2, 6; C. 0, 7, 10, 5, 2, 12;
D. 18, 12, 0, 6, 14, 24; E. 10, 0,
11, 5, 7, 6; F. 12, 18, 2, 0, 8, 24;
G. 9, 4, 11, 6, 1, 3; H. 20, 16, 10,
2, 4, 20; I. 8, 3, 10, 2, 12, 7;
J. 22, 8, 18, 16, 14, 10; K. 8, 2,
3, 10, 7, 6; L. 4, 22, 16, 12, 20, 8

Answer Key

PAGE 110
A. 9, 6, 1, 3, 7, 11; B. 6, 24, 18, 33, 12, 15; C. 12, 10, 6, 2, 5, 0; D. 6, 0, 12, 3, 36, 27; E. 5, 10, 4, 0, 3, 8; F. 27, 12, 21, 3, 33, 30; G. 1, 3, 4, 8, 11, 9; H. 18, 9, 33, 21, 24, 30; I. 7, 2, 5, 2, 4, 12; J. 15, 21, 36, 9, 27, 0; K. 7, 0, 3, 5, 6, 10; L. 15, 3, 36, 18, 12, 9

PAGE 111
A. 10, 1, 0, 11, 2, 9; B. 36, 4, 20, 40, 48, 28; C. 3, 7, 2, 9, 12, 5; D. 16, 0, 8, 32, 48, 28; E. 7, 2, 3, 5, 1, 12; F. 32, 0, 44, 12, 8, 40; G. 1, 6, 0, 8, 10, 4; H. 44, 4, 24, 12, 40, 20; I. 4, 8, 9, 6, 7, 10; J. 32, 8, 44, 16, 20, 24; K. 7, 11, 4, 12, 8, 5; L. 20, 36, 8, 24, 32, 44

PAGE 112
A. 10, 11, 2, 1, 12, 9; B. 20, 10, 60, 55, 5, 45; C. 9, 4, 5, 11, 12, 1; D. 30, 0, 15, 5, 45, 55; E. 2, 0, 8, 6, 4, 1; F. 40, 0, 20, 15, 50, 30; G. 7, 5, 4, 8, 2, 11; H. 60, 25, 35, 10, 50, 40; I. 3, 8, 5, 4, 7, 9; J. 25, 15, 35, 5, 55, 60; K. 1, 3, 0, 6, 9, 10; L. 20, 40, 55, 25, 5, 50

PAGE 113
A. 1, 2, 10, 7, 0, 5; B. 66, 12, 30, 6, 48, 36; C. 4, 11, 2, 12, 6, 9; D. 48, 12, 36, 66, 30, 72; E. 6, 4, 12, 3, 10, 8; F. 54, 60, 48, 30, 18, 24; G. 0, 10, 8, 1, 11, 5; H. 18, 6, 24, 48, 60, 42; I. 8, 11, 6, 9, 7, 0; J. 42, 6, 72, 36, 54, 0; K. 7, 2, 5, 3, 12, 4; L. 0, 54, 42, 12, 24, 6

PAGE 114
A. 1, 11, 8, 6, 12, 3; B. 49, 63, 0, 21, 7, 77; C. 12, 4, 2, 5, 8, 9; D. 56, 70, 7, 21, 42, 77; E. 10, 7, 9, 2, 4, 5; F. 56, 0, 35, 21, 84, 14; G. 11, 6, 1, 7, 3, 2; H. 14, 84, 56, 42, 0, 35; I. 3, 0, 12, 1, 9, 10; J. 14, 42, 70, 63, 28, 49; K. 1, 0, 10, 4, 5, 6; L. 21, 49, 28, 63, 14, 70

PAGE 115
A. 5, 4, 6, 1, 0, 8; B. 88, 16, 40, 8, 64, 48; C. 2, 12, 6, 8, 4, 5; D. 72, 8, 96, 80, 56, 24; E. 12, 8, 3, 10, 7, 5; F. 72, 80, 64, 40, 24, 32; G. 1, 7, 9, 10, 0, 11; H. 88, 64, 32, 0, 8, 72; I. 6, 10, 9, 11, 4, 2; J. 56, 8, 96, 48, 72, 0; K. 10, 8, 2, 11, 3, 1; L. 96, 32, 40, 16, 24, 48

PAGE 116
A. 1, 9, 7, 8, 0, 4; B. 9, 81, 63, 54, 0, 99; C. 4, 6, 5, 1, 0, 9; D. 18, 90, 108, 54, 36, 72; E. 5, 8, 3, 11, 9, 12; F. 54, 45, 90, 36, 63, 27; G. 8, 3, 7, 11, 12, 4; H. 99, 27, 0, 63, 18, 45; I. 4, 10, 0, 2, 3, 6; J. 36, 99, 108, 45, 18, 72; K. 10, 1, 0, 8, 6, 2; L. 9, 0, 81, 90, 63, 27

PAGE 117
A. 2, 8, 0, 7, 11, 9; B. 90, 40, 20, 100, 70, 120; C. 0, 5, 8, 9, 12, 7; D. 110, 60, 90, 70, 120, 80; E. 12, 4, 8, 6, 3, 1; F. 80, 30, 10, 60, 20, 0; G. 4, 11, 6, 10, 3, 8; H. 30, 20, 60, 100, 90, 50; I. 9, 1, 3, 10, 5, 2; J. 120, 60, 110, 0, 10, 50; K. 12, 6, 5, 1, 11, 2; L. 70, 50, 40, 10, 0, 80

PAGE 118
A. 7, 2, 11, 10, 0, 1; B. 11, 0, 66, 44, 55, 99; C. 1, 8, 5, 9, 11, 12; D. 121, 99, 132, 66, 55, 88; E. 5, 6, 4, 7, 11, 8; F. 33, 22, 77, 121, 110, 55; G. 5, 3, 7, 4, 6, 9; H. 33, 110, 121, 66, 22, 99; I. 12, 3, 9, 2, 10, 6; J. 121, 44, 22, 88, 0, 132; K. 10, 5, 2, 6, 0, 3; L. 55, 77, 11, 110, 0, 33

PAGE 119
A. 7, 12, 6, 1, 3, 5; B. 36, 0, 96, 84, 72, 132; C. 5, 8, 2, 9, 7, 10; D. 108, 48, 0, 144, 96, 132; E. 11, 10, 4, 9, 0, 6; F. 24, 120, 60, 12, 96, 48; G. 4, 6, 11, 3, 12, 9; H. 72, 12, 60, 84, 0, 120; I. 8, 4, 11, 2, 9, 3; J. 36, 132, 108, 0, 144, 60; K. 10, 3, 5, 6, 0, 1; L. 36, 120, 48, 96, 24, 84

PAGE 120
A. 12, 7, 11, 9, 8, 6; B. 21, 48, 48, 6, 25, 72; C. 5, 7, 8, 4, 10, 11; D. 30, 96, 9, 35, 60, 63; E. 6, 5, 7, 10, 12, 5; F. 72, 24, 9, 36, 70, 36; G. 4, 0, 6, 8, 5, 9; H. 55, 16, 4, 32, 10, 10; I. 4, 7, 9, 5, 11, 3; J. 110, 56, 0, 24, 54, 18; K. 12, 7, 11, 2, 9, 4; L. 12, 64, 27, 60, 77, 8

PAGE 121
A. 2, 8, 12, 3, 10, 10; B. 40, 28, 12, 66, 12, 40; C. 7, 5, 2, 11, 5, 3; D. 45, 88, 12, 132, 100, 28; E. 11, 4, 6, 10, 12, 0; F. 24, 108, 110, 0, 18, 24; G. 8, 12, 3, 9, 5, 2; H. 18, 8, 20, 14, 99, 54; I. 9, 1, 12, 12, 11, 8; J. 15, 120, 81, 36, 10, 84; K. 10, 11, 2, 8, 9, 12; L. 60, 16, 90, 36, 5, 144